PESHAṬ

(Plain Exegesis)

in

TALMUDIC AND MIDRASHIC LITERATURE

THIS THESIS WAS ACCEPTED FOR THE PH.D. DEGREE

AT

DUBLIN UNIVERSITY,

IRELAND

PESHAṬ

(Plain Exegesis)

in

TALMUDIC AND MIDRASHIC LITERATURE

by

RABBI DR. ISRAEL FRANKEL

EVALUATION BY

RABBI LEO JUNG, M.A., PH.D., D.D., D.H.L.

FOREWORD BY

R. TRAVERS HERFORD, M.A., D.D., D.H.L.

TORONTO

LA SALLE PRESS

1956

PRINTED IN CANADA

TYPOGRAPHY BY

PARAMOUNT TYPESETTING CO.

TO MY WIFE,
SONS AND DAUGHTERS
In love and affection

A man's wife is his home,
Yoma, 2a.
His children are his builders,
Berachoth, end.

PREFACE

This volume is the first of what is anticipated will be, a series of treatises which, it is hoped, will also embrace a running commentary on several of the books of the Bible, on the lines and method presented in the appendix of this issue.

In sending forth this book, I express the hope that it will assist students of Rabbinics to attain a better understanding of Rabbinic exegesis in general and particularly a fuller appreciation of Peshaṭ, plain exegesis, in Talmudic and Midrashic literature.

It is a pleasure for me to acknowledge my gratitude to many colleagues and friends for useful suggestions and helpful encouragement.

I am especially indebted to my esteemed friend and counsellor Professor Dr. Joshua Baker, Lecturer in Hebrew at Trinity College, Dublin, Ireland, for his valued advice and guidance in the preparation and execution of this work. I am grateful to him for the deep and constant interest he manifested in the progress of the book during the long period of study and research.

My warmest thanks are due also to Dr. J. Weingreen, Professor of Hebrew at the same College, for his help on the grammatical section of Ch. V.

ISRAEL FRANKEL

Adar, 5715
March, 1955,
Toronto

TABLE OF CONTENTS

Key to the Abbreviations
Evaluation by Rabbi Leo Jung
Foreword by R. Travers Herford
Introduction
1 Rabbinic Exegesis—Conflicting Opinions
2 Origin and Development of Rabbinic Exegesis
3 Rabbinic Exegesis in Relation to Peshaṭ
4 The Rabbis and the Study of the Bible
5 The Rabbis' Appreciation of Peshaṭ
Appendix
Rabbinic Sources
List of Works Referred to

KEY TO ABBREVIATIONS

(1) *Books of the Bible*

Gen.	Genesis.
Ex.	Exodus.
Lev.	Leviticus.
Num.	Numbers.
Deut.	Deuteronomy.
Josh.	Joshua.
Jud.	Judges.
1 and 2 Sam.	First and second Samuel.
1 and 2 King.	First and second Kings.
1and 2 Chron.	First and second Chronicles.
Is.	Isaiah.
Jer.	Jeremiah.
Ezek.	Ezekiel.
Am.	Amos.
Hag.	Haggai,
Zech.	Zechariah.
Mal.	Malachi.
Ps.	Psalms.
Prov.	Proverbs.
Koh.	Koheleth.
Lam.	Lamentations.

(2) *Rabbinic Sources*

Gen. R.	Genesis Rabbah.
Ex. R.	Exodus Rabbah.
Lev. R.	Leviticus Rabbah.
Num. R.	Numbers Rabbah.
Deut. R.	Deuteronomy Rabbah.
Mek.	Mekilta.
Tanḥ.	Tanḥuma.
J.	Jerushalmi.
Ber.	Berakoth.
Shab.	Shabbath.
Erub.	Erubin.
Pes.	Pesaḥim.
Beẓ.	Beẓah.
Suk.	Sukkah.
R. Hash.	Rosh Hashanah.
Taan.	Ta'anith.
Meg.	Megillah.
Ḥag.	Ḥagigah.
Yeb.	Yebamoth.
Keth.	Kethuboth.
Ned.	Nedarim.
Naz.	Nazir.
Giṭ.	Giṭṭin.
Ḳid.	Ḳiddushin.
B. Ḳamma.	Baba Ḳamma.
B. Meẓ.	Baba Meẓia.
B. Bath.	Baba Bathra.
Sanh.	Sanhedrin.
Sheb.	Shebuoth.
Mak.	Makkoth.
Ab. Zarah.	Abodah Zarah.

Zeb.	Zebaḥim.
Men.	Menaḥoth.
Ḥul.	Ḥullin.
Bek.	Bekoroth.
Ṭem.	Ṭemurah.
Ṭam.	Ṭamid.
Nid.	Nidah.

(3) *Versions*

A. V.	Authorised Version.
E. V.	English Version.
R. V.	Revised Version.
Pesh.	Peshitta.
Sam.	Samaritan.
Sept.	Septuagint.
Targ. Jon.	Targum Jonathan.
Targ. Onk.	Targum Onkelos.
Vulg.	Vulgate.

(4) *Miscellaneous*

a. e.	and elsewhere.
a. fr.	and frequently.
b.	ben.
ch.	chapter.
cf.	compare.
ed.	edition.
Heb.	Hebrew.
J. E.	Jewish Encyclopedia.
l. c.	locum citatum.
lect.	lecture.
Pent.	Pentateuch.
par.	paragraph.

R.	Rabbi.
s.v.	sub voce.
vol.	volume.

TRANSLITERATION OF HEBREW WORDS

בּ, ב	by	b	י	by	y
ה	"	h	כ	"	k
ז	"	z	צ	"	ẓ
ח	"	ḥ	ק	"	ḳ
ט	"	ṭ	ת	"	t

EVALUATION

by

RABBI LEO JUNG

M.A., Ph.D., D.D., D.H.L.

The problem of *Peshaṭ* in relation to *Derash* and *Halakah* has occupied the minds of our scholars for milennia. My sainted teacher, the Gaon David Hoffman, made great contributions to the subject, both in the introduction to his monumental work on Leviticus and in his basic "*Einleitung in die halachischen Midraschim*". Dr. Frankel set himself the task of providing evidence that the sages of the Talmud and Midrash, the large margin of individual interpretation notwithstanding, had a clear knowledge of the simple meaning of the text and of its primary importance in the interpretation of Holy Scripture. From a comprehensive and painstaking study the author is able to furnish some important material which should cause scholars to revise their notions as to the "strangeness, extravaganzas and homiletical adventures of rabbinic scholars" in their treatment of the text of the Hebrew Bible.

Dr. Frankel establishes beyond a shadow of a doubt that knowledge of the Holy text was general even among non-scholars in the Jewish community; that the Disciples of the Wise studying the lines and between the lines of Holy Writ, and engaged in detailed as well as in general systematized deep research, not only were fully familiar with the nuances and the problems of Hebrew grammar, but that the Peshaṭ was the single basis of their work. They knew the significance of Peshaṭ. Their dedicated study of every letter of the Holy text, their penetration into variations of meaning through comparison, for the elicitation of every possible meaning, of similar passages and cognate statements, their study of synonyms from Midrash Rabbah down to last century's Malbim, all were predicated on the understanding that embellishments are interesting and some straining of the text may result in occasional further exhaustion of the well-nigh bottomless implications of the Holy words, but that with all ingenuity and all the finesses of *Derash*, *Remez*, and *Sod* (inferential or mystic lore) the simple meaning may never be either ignored or denied its abiding significance. Just as freedom of interpretation of the Tenakh, with all liberality, does not permit interference with the objective validity of the Halakha, so does the privilege and duty to include all possible shades of meaning for an *ad hoc* teaching, a historical parallel, a moral principle, never impinge upon the objective authority of the simple text.

Dr. Frankel makes that abundantly clear and deserves every commendation both for his thorough workmanship as well as for his exhaustive quest. As to the relation of *Peshaṭ* to *Halakah*, several ingenious attempts have been made in the last and in our century by the sainted great Bible commentator, M. L. Malbim and the Gaon Moses Amiel respectively, both revealing extraordinary learning and keenness of method. But I have remained unconvinced by these learned efforts to establish a grammar of Halakah.

I feel sure that every serious student will accept Dr. Frankel's book with satisfaction and gratitude. He has finally destroyed the glib assurance of scholars Jewish and non-Jewish, who had words, as harsh as unjustified, to say about the "disrespect of rabbinic scholars for the plain meaning of the text". He has shown up the superficiality of their broad hints that such disrespect may have been founded by insufficient familiarity with either language or grammar.

In the course of his fine study, the author manages to convey a great deal of *en passant* knowledge which adds to the pleasure and profit derivable from the perusal of his book. His references are as wide as they are well-chosen and they do establish a thorough justification of his main argument.

Nissan, 5715
April, 1955

FOREWORD

by

REV. R. TRAVERS HERFORD

B.A., D.D., D.H.L.

It is with great pleasure that, at the request of the author, I write these lines as a foreword to his book. I have read it carefully through, and the impression which it has made upon me is that of a sound and scholarly piece of work. It is, moreover, a real contribution to the study of the Rabbinic literature. It deals with a problem which, as far as I know, has not hitherto been made the subject of special study, the problem of the plain exegesis (Peshaṭ) of the Scriptures, the literal meaning of what is there recorded, and the way in which the Rabbis regarded that literal meaning.

This is a real problem, deserving of careful study, because, in the Rabbinical literature, which is nearly all interpretation of Scripture, the exegesis in very many passages departs widely from the literal meaning, peshaṭ, and obtains results which seem to have no connection with the underlying text. It is on the evidence of such exegesis that the Talmud and cognate literature have been held up to scorn as trivial or charged with being blasphemous, in any case not worth the notice of readers who wish to ascertain the real sense of Scripture. There would, of course, have been no such problem if the writers who pronounced such unfavourable judgments had really understood what the Rabbis intended, when they devised a form of exegesis (Midrash) so different from the Peshaṭ. It is mostly (though not entirely) Gentile ignorance that is responsible for this abuse of the Talmud. But the Rabbis did not shape the form of their teaching to suit the ideas of Gentiles, nor did they explain to the outsider their methods and principles. So the Gentiles had to flounder in their ignorance, not realising that serious students of the Bible, such as the Rabbis were, would not devote their lives to producing extravagant nonsense; and that if their own study of the Talmud ended in a *reductio ad absurdum,* there must be some flaw in their reasoning, or an insecure foundation for it.

The real foundation on which the whole of the Rabbinical literature was built up was the study of Torah (including all the Scripture) and the setting forth of what was taught therein. The Rabbis set out to learn and to teach. What they had to teach was what they found in the Torah, and they looked to no other source of instruction. In such intensive study of Scripture the devout student would find that many thoughts came into his mind as the result of meditating on some text, and such thoughts would remain associated with that text, though he hardly knew whether the text had suggested the thoughts or was only a helpful reminder of them. The whole of the Rabbinic literature is the result of such close study and devout meditation, concentrated on Torah, and filled with the desire to learn and set forth even more of its divine meaning. In study so carried on, two things are to be noted; first, that the interpretation must often widely exceed the limits of the literal meaning; and second, that the literal meaning was absolutely necessary as the foundation on which to base the further exposition.

And here we come to the real value and importance of the book now commended to the reader. The author has shown by a multitude of examples, arranged with great skill, that the Rabbis not only knew their Scriptures in every detail, but took account of the plain meaning, in all their expositions. They did not always explicitly refer to it (having something other to set forth), any more than Einstein mentions the four rules of arithmetic when setting forth the theory of relativity. So it was well done of our author to take this subject of Peshaṭ and set forth what there really is to it.

All students of the Rabbinical literature should welcome this book, and to their careful study I commend it.

—R. TRAVERS HERFORD.

Kelsall, Chester.
September, 1949.

INTRODUCTION

A history of Jewish interpretation of the Scriptures is yet to be written. It would require a lifetime of work and the space of many volumes. My theme is actually 'Rabbinic interpretation', covering, roughly speaking, a thousand years, from the days of Ezra 457 B.C.E., to the period of the last of the Amoraim, Rabina, who completed the redaction of the Babylonian Talmud in 499 C.E. This volume deals specifically with only one aspect of Rabbinic interpretation, namely 'Peshaṭ' (plain exegesis) in Talmudic and Midrashic literature, the problem being whether the Rabbis appreciated the simple meaning of the text of the Bible.

According to Jewish tradition,[1] as stated in Talmud and Midrash, the written Law received by Moses, was accompanied and complemented by an 'explanatory' oral law, which was transmitted throughout the succeeding generations. This tradition was also recognized by the writers of the Apocrypha, Philo, and the Church Fathers.[2]

The substance of this Oral Law included all that the Scribes, and the later Rabbis could deduce from the written Torah by means of specific exegetical interpreta-

---

1 Cf. infra ch. 2 note 10.
2 Cf. infra ch. 2 note 11.

tions and logical principles.[3] In other words, the full extent of the Rabbinical teachings, 'in outline', and the rules according to which they might be developed, existed side by side with the written Law throughout the generations.[4]

In fact, from the inherent character of the Bible, many passages being very briefly worded, others being on the face of them almost unintelligible, the existence of an oral law becomes a logical conclusion.

It was the spirit of this Oral Law that permeated the heart of the Jew and inspired him to manifest his unshaken fidelity to the Word of God. It was this Oral Law that moulded the Jew into what he is and what he will be, and enabled him to endure the trials of martyrdom throughout the ages.

After the Return from Babylon a spiritual revival took place, the study of the Torah was intensified. The Jewish way of life, based on the written Law in accordance with the 'traditional interpretation', was established on an elevated and firm basis.

But after Judea fell under the rule of Alexander the Great, in 332 B.C.E., the new Hellenic material civilization, already adopted by the surrounding nations, exercised its influence on Jewish life too. Indeed, the upper classes of the Jewish people deliberately assimilated the Hellenic culture.

---

3 Cf. Meg. 19b; J. Peah 2, 4. Cf. also Ber. 5a; Yoma 28b and Rashi ad loc.

4 Cf. infra p. 46.

Later, when Hellenistic influence had gradually penetrated from the periphery of Jewish national life to its fundamental ideals, the nation was ranged into two parties: an advanced Hellenizing section of aristocrats, and a stubborn core of the people bitterly opposed to Hellenism, and sincerely loyal to the Jewish Law. The struggle of the conflicting civilizations, Hellenism and Judaism, reached its climax with the Maccabean revolt after which the two major sections within the Jewish fold—the Pharisees and the Sadducees—came into being.

The Pharisees stood for the development of Jewish tradition on its own lines and for separation from all denationalizing influence. Positively, they were the upholders of the Torah and expanders of its 'Interpretation in accordance with the tradition', and negatively, they were the opponents of alien ideas.

The Sadducees, as over against them, were the aristocratic party, which to a great degree inherited the outlook of the former Hellenists. They cherished the ambition to play a part in the affairs of the East. This ambition seemed to them attainable through imitation of Greek manners and through narrowing Judaism to a 'fixed creed as contained in the Bible' and to a 'rigid conservative Law'. It was the Sadducees who, for the first time in Jewish history, as a section of the Jewish people, assailed the mode of traditional exposition of the Scriptures.

For almost two thousand years thereafter the Talmud and other Rabbinic literature, which on the whole are merely 'interpretation of the Bible', were subjected to persecution in the literal sense of the word. The methods of persecution, however, varied in accordance with the times and circumstances.

Down the ages, the real motive behind persecution of the Talmud was disguised as objection to the supposedly incorrect Rabbinical exposition of the Scriptures. The actual motive, however, was an ulterior one, traceable to the fact that Rabbinic teaching and its mode of exposition would not tolerate any approach to the Scriptures which was foreign to the true spirit of Judaism.

This becomes evident when we consider the fact, a bitter irony of history, that the persecutors of the Talmud originated actually from Israel's own loins, from sections animated with non-Jewish ideals.

The first attempts to destroy Talmudic teaching were made even before its compilation and completion as a book. It goes back, as outlined above, to the days of Antiochus Epiphanes, nearly two centuries B.C.E., when the Sadducees joined forces with the Samaritans and with the ruling foreign power against Rabbinic teaching.

Later, when the Jewish founders of Christianity publicly broke with the Pharisees, they too worked hand in hand with the Sadducees and Bothusians bitterly opposing their common enemy, 'Rabbinic interpretation of the Bible'. Among themselves, however, they differed widely in their approach to the interpretation of the Scriptures.

During succeeding generations, once Christianity had established itself as an entirely new religion quite distinct from Judaism, there was no danger of Christian influence on Judaism. The old arguments, however, between the

Sadducees and the Pharisees had never entirely died down. Since the days of the Temple there had always been groups of Jews who, because of tendencies to assimilate with the surrounding neighbours, opposed the teachings of the Rabbis and their mode of interpretation of the text of the Bible. This was one of the main factors that paved the way for the Karaite movement.

About the year 760 C.E., Anan Ben David, anxious to succeed his uncle Solomon as Exilarch, was not elected because of his known hostility to the Talmud. In revenge, he publicly took the field as an opponent of Rabbinic interpretation of the text, claiming to be a strict adherent of the letter of the written word.

Thereupon, he attracted to his side the various Jewish sects who took their stand on the Bible alone, and united the opponents of Rabbinic interpretation in one strong body. Thus the Karaite sect was founded—a sect which was antagonistic to the Rabbis for centuries thereafter.

From what has been indicated above one can hardly suggest that the opponents of Rabbinic interpretation were ever genuinely concerned with the true meaning of the text of the Bible. It was rather deliberate malice on the part of both, the Sadducees and the Jewish founders of Christianity, that prompted their bitter fight against the Oral Law. They realized that this Oral Law nourished national consciousness within the Jew and that it fostered an aversion to whatever was not true to the cardinal points of Judaism.

The Sadducees, on the one hand, in fanatically adhering to the 'letter' in the strictest sense of the word, sought to destroy the 'spirit' of the Torah. Christianity, on the other hand, in following Hellenistic allegorism and putting the emphasis on symbolism only, ignored the literal sense of the word altogether and threatened the 'letter', i.e. the functioning of the Torah.

The Rabbis, in order to protect the purity of the 'spirit' of the Divine teaching from any admixture of foreign elements, retained their hold upon the 'letter' (Peshaṭ) i.e. the literal sense of the word.

Thus the Rabbis strongly warned against any extreme tendencies in the interpretation of the text of the Bible. Against 'literalism', on the one hand, they say: "If one translates a verse literally, he is a liar",[5] and, on the other hand, against subjecting the text to 'allegorism' or 'symbolism' only, they say: "A Biblical verse can never lose its literal sense".[6]

Nevertheless, Rabbinic exegesis has been constantly accused, by ancient and even modern Gentile scholars, of "fantastic letter worship" and "ignorance of the spirit",[7] a charge which cannot stand any critical examination.

In fact if we only consider the important role that Midrash played in Rabbinic literature, the absurdity of this accusation is evident, since "the term Midrash desig-

---

5 Ḳid. 49a. Cf. infra p. 88.

6 Shab. 63a; Yeb. 11b and Yeb. 24a. Cf. Yeb. 24a, where Raba distinctly states that this principle applies to the "whole Torah". Cf. infra ch. 3 note 87.

7 Cf. F. W. Farrar, 'History of Interpretation', London, 1886, p. 13 and p. 22. Cf. M. L. Margolis, 'The Scope and Methodology of Biblical Philology', J.Q.R.N.S. Vol. 1 p. 28. Cf. W. H. Saulez, 'Romance of the Hebrew Language', p. 39.

nates an exegesis which, going more deeply than the mere literal sense, attempts to penetrate into the spirit of the Scriptures".[8] However, we shall furnish the reader with a few striking examples from Halakic and from Haggadic interpretation.

1. The Biblical maxim "An eye for an eye and a tooth for a tooth",[9] is interpreted by the Rabbis[10] to mean due compensation with money, in contrast to the Sadducees who adhering to the 'bare letter', required the literal execution of this law.[11]

2. The prohibitions against leaving one place on the seventh day[12] and against kindling fire on the Sabbath,[13] were interpreted by the Rabbis[14] so as to render the Sabbath "a delight", a day of social and spiritual joy and elevation. The Samaritans, however, and later the Karaites, who were in many ways followers of the Sadducean teachings, observed these prohibitions quite literally, remained confined to their homes, deprived themselves

---

8 J.E., Vol. 8, p. 548.

9 Ex. 21, 24.

10 B. Ḳamma 84a; cf. Ibn Ezra, RaMBaN and M. Mendelssohn ad loc. Cf. J. H. Hertz, on Ex. 21, 24 and in the additional notes on Ex.

11 S. Horovitz, J.E. s.v. Midrash, observes: "The well-known interpretation of the passage "an eye for an eye", contradicting the view of the Sadducees, who wished to apply the law literally, gives evidence of a free and profound conception of the Biblical text even at that early date".

12 Ex. 16, 29.

13 Ex. 35, 3.

14 Cf. Shab. 70a; Erub. 17b and 51a; Yeb. 6b and Sanh. 35b. Cf. J. H. Hertz on Ex. 35, 3.

even of heat and light, thereby imposing upon the day of Sabbath a tone of utter gloom.

3. In the text "Ye shall therefore keep My statutes, and Mine ordinances, which if a man do, he shall live by them",[15] the Rabbis[16] take the words "he shall live by them", to mean that God's commandments are to be a means of life and not of destruction. With the exception of three prohibitions—murder, idolatry and adultery[17]—all commandments of the Law, are, therefore, in abeyance whenever life is endangered.[18]

4. The text just mentioned, which contains that important Halakic interpretation of וחי בהם ולא שימות בהם, also contains an Haggadic interpretation, which like the previous examples, illustrates in just as striking a way the profound conception and free handling of the text of the Bible by the Rabbis.

"Ye shall therefore keep My statutes, and Mine ordinances which if a man do, he shall live by them". The Rabbis,[19] empahisizing the word 'man', say: "Whence do we know that even a heathen, if he obeys the law of God, will thereby attain to the same spiritual communion with God as the High Priest? Scripture says, 'which if a man

15 Lev. 18, 5.

16 Yoma 85b; Sanh. 74a. Cf. Ab. Zarah 54a; J. Taanith 4, 5.

17 Cf. Sanh. 74a.

18 In order to duly appreciate the important role this Halakic interpretation played in Jewish life, and its tremendous influence on the development of Judaism in general, we must bear in mind the wars of extermination waged against Judaism throughout the generations.

19 B. Ḳamma 38a.

do, he shall live by them'—not Priest, Levite or Israelite, but 'man' ".

These four examples, picked at random, speak for themselves in reply to the accusations of "fantastic letter worship" and "ignorance of the spirit" made against Rabbinic exegesis.

Indeed the 'letter' and 'spirit' of the Scriptures, were conceived by the Rabbis of the Talmud and Midrash, as 'body' and 'soul'. Though one cannot exist without the other, nevertheless, just as the 'body' is to serve the 'soul' so is the 'letter' meant to serve the 'spirit'—the spirit of the Divine teaching. As M. Gudeman says:[20] "the Jewish teachers felt themselves compelled to retain their hold upon the letter, not for the sake of the letter, but for the sake of the spirit".

On the other hand, the Rabbis of the Talmud and Midrash, have also been accused of not having appreciated 'Peshaṭ', i.e. the plain meaning of the text of the Bible. Rabbinic interpretation has been ridiculed, and condemned for being incorrect and even false. These accusations arise from investigations which are both superficial and cursory.

Because of this unjustified criticism there developed against Rabbinic teaching a spirit of prejudice, even among the general reading public, both Jews and Gentiles alike. This is not surprising, since the Talmud and Midrash are subjects they have often heard of, but of which they, as a rule, unfortunately know little.

---

20 J.Q.R.O.S. Vol. 4, 'Spirit and Letter in Judaism and Christianity.'

It is in the hope of dispelling the ignorance that prevails in many circles concerning Rabbinic interpretation, that this very pleasurable task has been undertaken. If this volume aids in clearing up this misunderstanding, it will not have been written in vain.

Before concluding the introductory remarks, we wish to state emphatically our firm conviction, that behind the Haggadic interpretation there is always a basic conception of the simple sense. It is the discovery of the 'Peshaṭ' behind the 'Midrash' that we have in mind. Throughout the fabric of Rabbinic interpretation runs the unifying principle, already referred to, that "A Biblical verse can never lose its literal sense".[21]

And let it be said here, that the modern scientific exegesis is, both indirectly and sometimes even directly, derived from traditional Rabbinic interpretation. Indeed the ancient versions are the outcome of Jewish exegesis. Rashi, Ibn Ezra and Ḳimḥi, whose exegesis was widely influential and dominated the interpretation of the Hebrew Bible for almost the last thousand years,[22] were themselves an expression of the continuity of the Targum, and Talmudic and Midrashic exegesis.

Pointing to the fact that modern non-Jewish exegetes fail to acknowledge their indebtedness to the old Jewish masters of Biblical science, and how, when Jewish authorities are mentioned by them, they are dismissed with

21 Cf. infra ch. 3 notes 81, 86 and 87.

22 It is a well known fact that Luther was influenced by Rashi, and the Authorized Version is simply saturated with Rabbinic exegesis.

irony at their 'Rabbinic conceits' M. H. Segal, makes the following observation:[23]

"Even so just and generous a scholar as the late Professor Driver could bring himself to cite 'the Jews' with a contemptuous smile (see his note on 1 Sam. 18, 21). 'The Jews' in this particular case happen to be none other than the great Rabbi David Ḳimḥi, the original fountain-head of Hebrew learning in the Protestant church, who is reproduced by Professor Driver in his very next note, as in numerous other passages in his admirable work, without, however, the least acknowledgment".

Finally, to those who have so much to say about Rabbinic interpretation, we say: "The Talmud is the commentary on the Torah; the outcome, not of theory, but of life and action. It is a commentary on the revealed Law, based on the actual observance of its precepts; the endeavour to satisfy, in both letter and spirit, the Divine commandments".[24]

And "surely a poet is the poet's best interpreter and philosopher the philosopher's. In the same manner it requires a religious mind to understand psalmist and prophet, and only he that is nurtured by Jewish thought, itself rooted in the Scriptures, may hope to master the Scriptural Word in its fullest and deepest import."[25]

---

23 J.Q.R.N.S. Vol. 10 P. 421.

24 Dudly Wright, 'The Talmud', conclusion.

25 M. L. Margolis, 'The Scope and Methodology of Biblical philology, J.Q.R.N.S. Vol. 1.

CHAPTER ONE

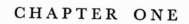

CHAPTER ONE

RABBINIC EXEGESIS— CONFLICTING OPINIONS

Having regard to the extensive scope and variety of its subject-matter, it is not surprising to find that Rabbinic literature has given rise to conflicting views about the opinions held by the Rabbis, particularly as regards their attitude to the interpretation of Scripture. Moreover, "Rabbinic literature is not an open book even for erudite students of the Bible, with the result that its bounteous legacy of knowledge and inspiration does not always receive the grateful recognition which it merits."[1] The Talmud and allied books, on the whole, being of intrinsic rather than extrinsic value, beautiful in essence yet harsh in form, in almost every respect exceptional, "are not easily accessible, still less-easily read, still less-easily understood when they are read".[2] Indeed, as E. Deutsch points out,[3] a certain Dominican, Henricus Seynensis, speaks of the Talmud as though of a person, thus: "As says Rabbi Talmud . . ."

---

1 From an unpublished work by J. Baker. See M. Mielziner 'Introduction to the Talmud', N.Y. 1925, 3rd ed. ch. 13.
2 R. T. Herford, 'Pharisees', London, 1924, p. 176.
3 E. Deutsch, 'Literary Remains', London, 1874, p. 3.

A number of non-Jewish scholars[4] who studied Rabbinic lore from its original sources have acknowledged the contribution of Rabbinic literature to an understanding of the Bible;[5] others, whose knowledge did not come direct from the fountain-head, frequently found themselves compelled to ridicule and reject Rabbinic exegesis; indeed some of them, however renowned, betray a complete misunderstanding of its basic features. W. R. Smith, for instance, states: "People often think of the Jews as entirely absorbed, from the very first, in the exact grammatical study and literal preservation of the written Word. Had it been so, they could never have devised so many expositions, which are plainly against the idiom of the language".[6] F. W. Farrar likewise errs in his approach to the subject, for he says: "The actual exegesis of Scripture in which the Talmud abounds is so arbitrary and so futile, so tasteless and so insincere, that it must have given to its students a radically false conception of their sacred books . . . What has been said of the Talmud applies in general to all the Rabbinic writings and to the

---

4 E.g., J. Lightfoot; the Buxtorfs; C. Taylor; A. C. Jennings; H. Strack; E. Robertson; R. T. Herford; H. Danby, etc. Cf. I. B. Levinsohn, 'Beth Yehudah', Warsaw, 1878, ch. 112 on this point.

5 A. C. Jennings, 'Prolegomena', to Ps. ch. 5, London, 1884, 2nd ed., states: "The most valuable source of exegesis is undoubtedly Rabbinic literature". See also S. Schechter, Introduction to 'Documents of Jewish Sectaries', Cambridge, 1910, and M. Mielziner, 'Introduction to the Talmud', N.Y., 1925, 3rd ed., ch. 13.

6 W. R. Smith, 'Old Testament in the Jewish Church', London, 1895, 2nd ed., Lect. 3.

whole collection of Midrashim".[7] Such denunciation, as I. Abrahams[8] explains, arises from the fact that Farrar's investigations were too superficial.

Even more surprising, such Jewish scholars as H. Graetz, I. H. Weiss and L. Zweifel (all well versed in the original Rabbinic sources) failed to grasp the true spirit of the Rabbis in their exegesis, and this led, to some extent, to the misunderstanding of Rabbinic exegesis which we find perpetuated in the monumental works of W. R. Smith, F. W. Farrar and others.[9] In his "History of the Jews", during the course of an apologetic review of the Talmud, H. Graetz remarks: "It favours a bad interpretation of Scripture, absurd, forced and frequently false commentations . . ."[10] thus giving the impression that the Rabbis did not understand Peshaṭ.[11] I. H. Weiss (followed by L. Zweifel)[12] likewise states: "All the interpretations given by the Rabbis—even such as are obviously opposed to the plain meaning—were regarded by

---

7 F. W. Farrar, 'History of Interpretation', London, 1886, pp. 94-95.

8 I. Abrahams, 'Rabbinic Aids to Exegesis', in 'Cambridge Biblical Essays', London, 1909.

9 E.g., S. Davidson (in his contribution in 'Kitto's Cyclopaedia of Biblical Literature', Edinburgh, 3rd ed. s.v. 'Talmud') who slavishly follows H. Graetz without acknowledgment.

10 H. Graetz, 'History of the Jews' (Heb. ed. S. P. Rabinovitz, Warsaw, 1893), vol. 2 p. 455. Translation of the above quotation is taken from M. Mielziner, 'Introduction to the Talmud', N.Y. 1925, 3rd ed., p. 106.

11 'Peshaṭ' (פשט)—plain interpretation of Scripture, contrasted with the free Midrashic treatment of the text. See infra p. 48.

12 L. Zweifel, 'Sanegor', Warsaw, 1885, p. 147.

them as Peshaṭ".[13] On the other hand, some authorities[14] went to the other extreme, viz. that every Rabbinic interpretation was intended to represent and in fact did represent the plain meaning of the Biblical text. They sought to show that every Rabbinic interpretation, however far-fetched, could be harmonised with the wording of Scripture.

Actually, this conflict of opinion is to be found throughout the history of exegesis. Of these two diametrically-opposed schools of thought Maimonides remarks: "Neither understood that our Sages employ Biblical texts merely as poetical expressions, the meaning of which is clear to every reasonable reader".[15]

The purpose of this work is to show that, while Rabbinic exegesis as recorded in Rabbinic literature frequently deviates from Peshaṭ,[16] with their extraordinary knowledge of the Bible the Rabbis had a clear appreciation of the plain meaning as distinct from the Midrash superimposed upon it; and in this connection, it will also be shown that interesting comments of objective value from the point of view of sound Biblical exegesis, abound in the Talmud and Midrashim.

---

13 I. H. Weiss, 'Dor', Wilna, 1911, vol. 1, ch. 18; cf. vol. 2, ch. 11 and his contribution in 'Kokebe Yiẓḥaḳ', No. 37 by M. Stern.

14 E.g., J. H. Mecklenburg in his 'Ha-Ketab weha-Ḳabbala', 4th ed., Frankfort a.M. 1880; and Malbim in his commentaries on the Bible, Mekilta, Sifra and Sifre.

15 Maimonides, 'Guide', M. Friedlander's translation, London, 1904, 2nd ed., part 3, ch. 43.

16 For reasons explained infra pp. 49-51, 57, 61, 63-71, 77-80.

CHAPTER TWO

CHAPTER TWO

ORIGIN AND DEVELOPMENT OF RABBINIC EXEGESIS

To essay even a general outline of the vast store of exegetical material embedded in the Talmud and Midrashim is outside the scope of this work. The Talmud has been said to comprise a "legal code, a system of ethics, a body of ritual customs, poetical passages, prayers, histories, facts of science and medicine and fancies of folklore".[1] The various collections of Midrashim, too, mirror the life, civilisation and culture of a people extending over a thousand years. Moreover, the greater part of Rabbinic literature had been transmitted orally by generations of scholars before being reduced to writing; the Mishnah was not compiled until the close of the second century, C.E., the Palestinian Talmud about the year 370, the Babylonian Talmud a century later, while some of the Midrashim did not receive permanent literary form until as late as the 10th or 11th century. Independent schools of thought, flourishing at different times and under varying conditions, to some extent influenced by the nations with whom the Jews came in contact, con-

---

1 I. Abrahams, 'The Talmud', in his 'Short History of Jewish Literature', London, 1906.

tributed to the creation of these monumental works. Occasionally we find two opposing schools flourishing at the same time; and if to all this we add the differences in outlook and opinion among the individual Rabbis of the same school, the difficulty of summarising the exegetical material in those works becomes apparent.

Despite the extensive range of subject-matter of Rabbinic literature, it may be said that that literature is concerned mainly with "the exegetic treatment of the Bible and the systematic development of the Law derived from it".[2]

From earliest times, the study of Torah[3] was the highest ideal among the Jews. "As the child must satisfy its hunger each hour, so must the grown man busy himself with the Torah each hour".[4] Sanctity, even prophylactic power, was ascribed to the study of the Torah.[5] The supreme importance of study, for its own sake, is emphasised thus: "The practice of all the laws of the Pentateuch is worth less than the study of the Scriptures of it."[6]

---

2 J. E. vol. 3, p. 162.

3 The word 'Torah' ('Teaching', 'Instruction', 'Law') defies translation. It is used for (a) Pentateuch (Written Law); (b) Mishnah (Oral Law); (c) The whole body of Jewish religious literature. See S. Schechter, 'Some Aspects of Rabbinic Theology', N.Y., 1909, p. 122; M. Friedlander, 'The Jewish Religion', London, 1937, p. 326; J.E., vol. 12, p. 129; S. Singer, 'The Authorised Daily Prayer Book', note on Aboth 1, 1; R. T. Herford, 'Pharisees', ch. 3 and 'Talmud and Apocrypha', London, 1933, p. 7. See infra pp. 47-8.

4 J. Ber. 9, 5. Cf. Shab. 30a; Erub. 63b; Meg. 16b, a. e.

5 Cf. Ber. 5a; Erub. 54a and b; Sanh. 98b and 99b, a.e.

6 J. Peah, 1, 1.

Yet the study of Torah also had a practical end. There, was to be found a guide for the people in everything affecting their daily life. The Torah was God's revelation to mankind; in the poetical language of the Haggadah, the Rabbis tell us: "God held counsel with the Torah at the creation of the world".[7]

It was on the basis of the divine origin of the Torah that the development of the religious and civil laws proceeded; in Scripture, particularly in the Pentateuch, were the answers sought. The Mishnah states: "Turn it (the Torah) and turn it over again, for everything is in it, and contemplate it, and wax grey and old over it, and stir not from it, for thou canst have no better rule than this".[8] This outlook is characteristic of Rabbinic thought, rooted in the very early traditions, particularly stressed since the fall of Jerusalem. With the dispersal of the people and the disintegration of their national life, the Rabbis of the "vineyard of Jamnia" (as that famous academy was called) sought to preserve Judaism by propagating a mode of life on the basis of Scripture and tradition, enforced by their moral authority. Throughout the fabric of Rabbinic Judaism runs the "unifying principle that literature in its truest sense includes life itself; that intellect is the handmaid to conscience; and that the best books are those which best teach men how to live".[9] This principle became one of the dominant factors in shaping the form and content of Rabbinic exegesis.

---

7 Gen. R. 1, 1; Tanḥ. Bereshith, 1.

8 Aboth, 5, 25.

9 I. Abrahams, Preface to 'Short History of Jewish Literature', London, 1906.

The importance of Scripture lay in that it prescribed a code of law and conduct sanctioned by divine teaching. In some instances where the Biblical text was silent on a particular point requiring a decision, the Rabbis had a "tradition" (קבלה) which enabled them to resolve the difficulty.

According to ancient Jewish tradition,[10] Moses received not only the written code, but also an accompanying oral law, explanatory and complementary, which was transmitted, throughout the generations.[11] This tradition, while exercising a profound influence on the development of Rabbinic exegesis, is not to be taken literally to mean that God imparted to Moses the whole of the Torah as developed in the course of time. As the Rabbis explain: "The forty days which Moses spent on Sinai would not have been sufficient for all that; the full extent of the Rabbinical teaching was, however, revealed to Moses in outline by giving him the rules according to which they might be developed".[12]

No code, of course, can cover all the varying circumstances of human life, and the Pentateuchal code is no exception. Even some of the express precepts contained

---

10 J. Peah, 2, 4; Ex. R. 47, 1; Ber. 5a.

11 The tradition as to the Oral Law is also recognised by the writers of the Apocrypha, Philo and the Church Fathers, cf. E. Deutsch, 'Literary Remains', London, 1874, p. 18; J.E. s.v. 'Oral Law'. Cf. S. Schechter, 'The History of Jewish Tradition', in 'Studies in Judaism', first series, Philadelphia, 1945.

12 Ex. R. 41, 6.

in the Pentateuch are incomplete in themselves.[13] For instance, we read that Moses did not know to which particular form of the death penalty the profaner of the Sabbath was liable; likewise in the case of the blasphemer, for we read: "They put him (the stick-gatherer) in ward, because it had not been declared what should be done to him".[14] "And they put him (the blasphemer) in ward, that it might be declared unto them at the mouth of the Lord".[15] The Prophets were the expounders and interpreters of many injunctions, e.g. Sacrifices,[16] Festivals,[17] Sabbath observance.[18] Exegesis in the wider sense is thus inherent in the Bible itself. "It was definitely not Rabbinic fanaticism that widened the implications of the words of the Bible; even long before the time of Ezra the term "Torah" denoted teaching given by or on behalf of God, the Communication of His Will or of whatever else He would make known to His people. This usage has been traced in the Pentateuch as well as in the Prophets".[19] The rendering by the Sept. of the word "Torah" into "Law" is incorrect, possibly a deliberate misread-

---

13 Cf. Ibn Ezra, Introduction to his Commentary on Pent., Method 2; I. Albo, 'Iḳḳarim', Warsaw, 1877, 3, 23; N. Krochmal, 'Moreh Nebuke ha-Zeman', Lemberg, 1863, Shaar 13; D. Nieto, Introduction to 'Cuzari Ḥeleḳ Sheni', London, 1714.

14 Num. 15, 34. Cf. Sifre 1.c. and Sanh. 78b.

15 Lev. 24, 12.

16 Amos 5, 21-4; Is. 1, 11-13; Jer. 7, 21-22; cf. Ps. 40, 7.

17 Is. 1, 14.

18 Is. 58, 13 (see interesting observation on Rabbinic exegesis regarding Sabbath observance by F. Delitzsch 1.c.); Jer. 17, 21; Neh. 13, 15.

19 R. T. Herford, 'Pharisees', ch. 3. Cf. S. Schechter, 'Some Aspects of Rabbinic Theology', N.Y., 1909, p. 116; M. Friedlander, Introduction to the 'Jewish Religion', London, 1937.

ing.[20] When the Mishnah tells us:[21] "Moses received the Torah on Sinai, and handed it down, etc." the word "Torah" was obviously meant to include more than the mere legislation found in the Pentateuch. It includes also the oral law already referred to.[22] A true appreciation of Rabbinic exegesis is impossible unless this fact—what the Rabbis understood by the term "Torah"—is clearly borne in mind.[23]

Interpretation thus becomes a process of supplementing the original record, generally known by the term "Midrash" (as distinct from Peshaṭ, "plain", interpretation) from the root "darash" to "investigate", i.e. in reference to the Bible, to "search out" or discern the meaning of the text. Traces of Midrash in this sense are to be found in the Bible itself.[24] "In contradistinction to the literal interpretation, subsequently called "Peshaṭ", the term "Midrash" designates an exegesis which, going more deeply than the mere literal sense, attempts to penetrate into the spirit of the Scriptures, to examine the text from all sides, and thereby to derive interpreta-

---

20 R. T. Herford, 'Pharisees', ch. 3; "Paul perpetuated the same mischievous error", ibid.

21 Aboth, 1, 1.

22 Cf. N. Krochmal, 'Moreh Nebuke ha-Zeman', Lemberg, 1863, Shaar 13; I. H. Weiss, 'Dor', vol. 1, ch. 6, contrary to Bacher in J.E., vol. 3, s.v. 'Bible Exegesis', according to whom the history of Jewish exegesis begins with Ezra's activities. Cf. S. Singer, 'The Authorised Daily Prayer Book', note on Aboth 1, 1.

23 See S. Schechter, 'Some Aspects of Rabbinic Theology', N.Y., 1909, p. 116 and R. T. Herford, 'Pharisees' ch. 3.

24 2 Chron. 13, 22; 24, 27; Ez. 7, 10. Cf. I. H. Weiss, 'Dor', Wilna, 1911, vol. 1, p. 159 and E. Deutsch, 'Literary Remains', London, 1874, p. 13.

tions which are not immediately obvious".[25] In the course of time, various rules of exegesis were formulated by the Rabbis, e.g. Hillel's[26] seven Rules, later extended to thirteen by R. Ishmael[27] and to thirty-two by R. Eliezer.[28] Some of these rules, though they undoubtedly serve as an aid to the understanding of the Biblical text, were not necessarily devised for that purpose.

The exegesis of the Midrash is divisible into two main categories, more or less mutually exclusive—Halakah and Haggadah. Halakah is chiefly concerned with the study and development of legal rules and precedents either associated with or exegetically derived from Scripture, particularly the legal portions of the Pentateuch. Haggadah is concerned with the exposition of Scripture, from the standpoint of religious, moral and ethical values. The extensive scope and content of the Haggadah is described by Zunz thus: "The Haggadah, which is intended to bring heaven down to the congregation, and also to lift man up to heaven, appears in this office both as the glorification of God and as the comfort of Israel. Hence religious truth, moral maxims, discussions concerning divine retribution, the inculcation of the laws which attest Israel's greatness, scenes and legends from Jewish history, comparisons between the divine and Jewish institutions, praises of the Holy Land, encouraging stories and comforting reflections of all kinds form the most important subjects of these discourses".[29]

25 J. E., vol. 8, p. 548.
26 About 30 B.C.—10 C.E.
27 At the end of 1st and beginning of 2nd C.
28 2nd C.
29 'G. V.'. Translation taken from J. E., vol. 8, p. 550.

Thus it is apparent that in the course of the development of Haggadah, religious edification, rather than elucidation of the true meaning of the Biblical text, became the keynote. The Haggadic discourses referred to by Zunz, representing the Haggadic art at its highest, undoubtedly sprang from a mode of treatment of the Biblical text, but so free is the treatment, at times so fanciful and so imaginative, so far removed from the ordinary meaning of the words, that these discourses, though valuable in their own way and serving their own admirable purposes, cannot be regarded as serious attempts as an exposition of the Biblical text. The same tendency is to be observed in the Halakah, though from the very nature of its subject-matter and the methods of interpretation bound up in the determination of legal rules, the Halakah was restricted by certain fixed Canons of interpretation, and as a result did not treat Scripture as freely and imaginatively as did the Haggadah. "The early Halakah, viz. that of the Soferim and the Tannaim of the first two generations, aims at an exact definition of the laws contained in Scripture by an accurate interpretation of the text and a correct determination of the various words. The form of exegesis adopted is frequently one of simple lexicography, and is remarkably brief".[30] But at the hands of the later Tannaim and their successors (the Amoraim) Halakic exegesis became much more flexible, going beyond a plain interpretation of the text.[31]

30 J.E. vol. 8, p. 570. Z. Frankel, 'Darke ha-Mishnah', Warsaw, 1923, p. 5, draws attention to the particular kind of exegesis found in the early Mishnah, viz. a quotation of the Biblical text with the addition of an occasional word or words.

31 Cf. J. E. ibid.

The reason is clear. The function of Halakah was to define the scope and meaning of particular rules, to associate new rules with the Biblical text and to reconcile apparent contradictions. If the Halakists tended to deviate from simple exegesis, it was not because they disapproved of it, but rather because that form of exegesis was inadequate for their purposes.

CHAPTER THREE

CHAPTER THREE

RABBINIC EXEGESIS IN RELATION TO PESHAṬ

To gain an insight into the intrinsic nature of Rabbinic exegesis in relation to Peshaṭ, it is necessary to consider the fundamental question: Was Midrashic exegesis intended by the Rabbis to convey the plain meaning of the Biblical text? That the greater part of Rabbinic exegesis does not do so is evident. Consider two typical interpretations, the first taken from the Halakah, the second from the Haggadah.

1. לא תהיה אחרי רבים לרעת ולא תענה על רִב לנטת אחרי רבים להטת "Thou shalt not follow a multitude to do evil; neither shall thou speak in a cause to turn aside after a multitude to wrest judgment".[1]

The word רִב in the second half of the verse is written without Yod. The Rabbis, interpreting the word as though it were written רַב (superior), expound the verse thus: "Thou shalt not speak against the chief (of the judges)"; in other words, the younger members of a criminal court must vote first so that their opinions may

1 Ex. 23, 2.

not be influenced by those of their older colleagues.[2] The verse is also quoted by the Rabbis as a basis for several other Halakoth. In this connection Rashi ad loc.[3] remarks: "There are Halakic interpretations of the verse given by the Sages of Israel, but the wording of the text does not fit in well with them".[4]

2. ויהי בשלח פרעה את העם ולא נחם אלהים דרך ארץ פלשתים "And it came to pass, when Pharaoh had let the people go, that God led them not by way of the land of the Philistines".[5]

The Rabbis appear to disregard the word פלשתים (Philistines) giving the expression דרך ארץ the secondary meaning it had acquired in Rabbinic literature viz. 'wordly manner', thus explaining the verse to mean: "God did not treat them (the children of Israel) in a worldly manner".[6]

Rabbinic literature abounds in examples of such exegesis, which does not interpret the text in its ordinary meaning. The problem for consideration is whether such interpretations were regarded by the Rabbis as inherent in the Biblical text or merely as superimposed.

We shall deal first with Halakah. According to Judah

---

2 Sanh. 36a. Cf. ibid 18b.

3 On Ex. 23, 2.

4 From the English translation of Rashi on the Pent. ed. by A. M. Silberman, London, 1930.

5 Ex. 13, 17.

6 Ex. R. 20, 11.

ha-Levi,[7] Abraham Ibn Ezra,[8] Moses Maimonides,[9] RABaD[10] (ראב"ד), D. Nieto,[11] Z. H. Chajes,[12] the Halakah did not result from Midrashic exegesis, but rather gave rise to it.[13] They trace the origin of most of the Halakic decisions to tradition, the Biblical text in many instances being supplied as an אסמכתא 'support' or רמז 'allusion' or זכר 'reminder'. In this view—adopted in this work and which for convenience may be termed the 'traditional'—it was because of the existence of the Halakah, for the purpose of giving it retroactive justification, that the text was construed in an artificial manner. On the other hand, some scholars consider that the Halakah arose from the Midrashic exegesis; according to this view—which will be referred to as the 'non-traditional'—the interpretations and deductions of the Rabbis appeared to them to be contained in the text, which they wished to be considered correct Biblical expositions. Among the

---

7 J. ha-Levi, 'Cuzari', Zamosc, 1796, 3, 73.

8 A. Ibn Ezra, 'Yesod Moreh', quoted by J. A. Moscato in 'Ḳol Yehudah', (Comm. on Cuzari) 3, 73.

9 Moses Maimonides, 'Sefer Hamitzvoth', shoresh 2; and in his 'Introduction' to the Mishnah.

10 Quoted by Nieto in the introduction to his 'Cuzari Ḥeleḳ Sheni', London, 1714.

11 D. Nieto, 'Cuzari Ḥeleḳ Sheni', in the first three Essays.

12 Z. H. Chajes, 'Introduction to the Talmud', Zolkiev, 1845, ch. 17.

13 See I. Halevy, 'Doroth ha-Rishonim', Frankfurt a.M. 1918, vol. 1e, pp. 467-522. According to him Nachmanides agrees with this view while Z. Frankel, 'Darke ha-Mishnah', Warsaw, 1923, ch. 1 and S. Horowitz, J.E. vol. 8, p. 548 consider Nachmanides as opposed to it.

followers of this view are Malbim,[14] I. H. Weiss,[15] Lauterbach[16] and S. Rosenblatt.[17] S. Horowitz[18] does not give a definite answer to the question, but the trend of his discussion favours the 'traditional' view. Let us examine the principal arguments in favour of the 'non-traditional' view, which may be summarised as follows:

1. The origin of the Halakah did not rest entirely on tradition; the manner in which a Biblical text is adduced in relation to a particular Halakah shows that the text was regarded as containing not merely an allusion to, but in fact, the actual Halakic interpretation itself. In support of this, attention is drawn to the mode of reasoning and deduction in the Halakic discussions in the Talmud in relation to the Biblical sources which are expounded in the context, e.g. such expressions as מנלן (whence do we have this?) or מנא הני מילי (whence are these words?), usually followed by the citation of the appropriate Biblical verse; or such expressions as דכתיב (as it is written) דאמר קרא (for Scripture says) or שנאמר (for it is said).[19]

2. "The fact that two or more constructions are put on the same expression is a sure indication that the

---

14 Malbim, 'Introduction' to Sifra.

15 I. H. Weiss, 'Dor', Wilna, 1911, vol. 1, ch. 18, and vol. 2, ch. 11.

16 J.E. vol. 8, p. 571.

17 S. Rosenblatt, 'Bible Interpretation in the Mishnah', Baltimore, 1935, p. 5.

18 J.E. vol. 8, p. 548. Cf. Z. Frankel, 'Darke ha-Mishnah', Warsaw, 1923, ch. 1.

19 See Malbim, 'Introduction to Sifra' and I. H. Weiss, 'Dor', Wilna, 1911, vol. 1, ch. 18.

Halakah or the Haggadah was the result of the exegesis or Midrash, not its cause".[20]

3. "Were the Biblical text quoted as an אסמכתא as the 'support' of a preconceived opinion, how does it happen that two divergent views derive their authority from the same source?"[21]

In considering these arguments, it is essential to bear in mind the different categories of Halakoth viz. (a) those expressly contained in the Bible; (b) arising from tradition and associated with a Biblical text; (c) not arising from tradition, but purporting to be derived from an exposition of the Biblical text; and finally (d) those which the Rabbis expressly enacted and which are clearly acknowledged by them as being independent, deliberate legislation not to be found in the Bible. The first three categories are known as דאורייתא (Biblical), the fourth as דרבנן (non-Biblical).

The short answer[22] to the first argument is that even in the case of those Halakoth דרבנן which the Rabbis regarded as non-Biblical, we find them employing the same kind of reasoning and argument, with the same kind of inquiries as to the Biblical source, in some discussions of this nature even stating at the conclusion: מדרבנן וקרא

20 S. Rosenblatt, 'Bible Interpretation in the Mishnah', Baltimore, 1935, p. 5, following Malbim, 'Introduction to the Sifra' and I. H. Weiss, 'Dor', vol. 1, ch. 18.

21 S. Rosenblatt ibid p. 5, following Malbim ibid and I. H. Weiss ibid.

22 In the ensuing discussion I am indebted, among many others, mainly to I. Halevy in his voluminous work, 'Doroth ha-Rishonim', Frankfurt a.M., 1901-1918.

אסמכתא בעלמא "It is actually a Rabbinical law, and the Bible text (quoted) is a mere 'support' *or mnemotechnical aid*".[23] E.g. טומאת עכו"ם (defilement of an idolatrous shrine) is introduced in the Mishnah [24] with the familiar expressions מניין and שנאמר and in the Gemara a very long discussion follows the same mode of reasoning as in the case of Halakoth דאורייתא. At the conclusion of the discussion[25] comes the definite statement that the origin of this law is 'דרבנן' only.

Similarly in the case of the law of תחום שבת (Sabbath limits of two thousand cubits in every direction), known to be a Rabbinical enactment,[26] the subject is introduced with the question הני אלפיים אמה היכן כתיבן (where is it written in Scripture the limits of the two thousand cubits?), a discussion supplying Biblical texts following.[27] Obviously, the Rabbis could not have expected to find in Scripture the source of these admittedly non-Biblical laws. Yet we find them groping around in search of a Biblical text.[28] Clearly, in such cases, the use of the Biblical text was not intended to involve the conclusion that the text itself contained the particular law, otherwise the law would necessarily have been regarded by the Rabbis as coming within one of the דאורייתא categories. Hence it would appear that, even in regard to such categories, the fact that a Biblical source was sought and found for them,

---

23 E. g. Yoma, 74a; Sanh. 83a; Ḥul. 64b a.e.
24 Shab. 9, 1; cf. Ab. Zarah 3, 6.
25 Shab. 83b.
26 See Rashi Shab, 34a, s.v. בעירובי תחומין.
27 Erub. 51b.
28 For another useful illustration see discussion in regard to בעל קרי in Ber. 21b; B. Ḳamma 82a; cf. Rashi on Mishnah Ber. 20b.

does not necessarily show that the law deduced therefrom or associated therewith was regarded by the Rabbis as inherent in the text.[29] In this connection C. Taylor remarks: "Rabbinic citations of Scripture are not intended always as absolute proofs of the doctrines and ideas in connection with which they are deduced".[30]

Of the Halakoth דאורייתא not expressly contained in the Bible, the majority arose from tradition;[31] the Halakoth purporting to be derived from the Biblical text are comparatively few. It is important to observe here that the traditional Halakoth are usually presented in the Mishnah without reference to any Biblical text as a source. Only in the later Rabbinic literature did the practice grow up of citing a Biblical verse in relation to such Halakoth.[32] A particular Halakah becomes associated with a verse but it is an association only. The citation of the verse does not mean that the Halakah depends upon the verse, or is derived from it. The relationship between the verse and the particular Halakah is more clearly seen in the following example: The Halakah with regard to setting free the mother of a nest of birds, is associated with Deut. 22, verses 6 and 7. Ac-

---

29 The purpose of such citations is dealt with infra pp. 66-9 a.e.

30 C. Taylor, 'Sayings of the Jewish Fathers', Cambridge, 1877, 3, 1. See S. Singer, 'The Authorised Daily Prayer Book', note on Aboth 3, 3.

31 Cf. infra pp. 64-9. See Maimonides, 'Introduction to the Mishnah'; Z. H. Chajes, 'Introduction to the Talmud', Zolkiev, 1845, ch. 17, and I. Halevy, 'Doroth ha-Rishonim', Frankfurt a.M., 1918, vol. 1e pp. 467-522.

32 See I. Halevy, 'Doroth ha-Rishonim', ibid.

cording to the Mishnah[33] this applies only to 'clean birds'. The Mishnah does not cite the passage in Deut., nor does it adduce any Biblical source for the exclusion of 'unclean birds'. In the Gemara,[34] however, we have the usual inquiry מנא הני מילי (Whence do we derive this law?), and in reply attention is drawn to Deut. 22, 6 viz. "If a bird's (צפור) nest chance to be before thee" where the term used is not עוף, which usually denotes both unclean as well as clean, but צפור, which denotes clean birds only. At first sight it would appear that the Halakah, as stated in the Mishnah, purports to be derived from the Biblical text. But an examination of the ensuing discussion in the Gemara[35] reveals that this is not so. Some of the Rabbinic authorities would seem to take the view that צפור denotes both classes of birds.[36] While such difference of opinion exists in the Gemara, it is important to note that the Halakic statement in the Mishnah is unanimous. It follows, therefore, that the Biblical text is cited merely by way of association with the particular Halakah, and not as its source.

This provides an effective answer not only to the first, but also to the second argument advanced in support of the 'non-traditional' view. But independently of these considerations, "the fact that many different constructions are put on the same text", far from supporting that

33 Ḥul. 12, 1.
34 Ḥul. 139b.
35 Ḥul. 140a.
36 According to Nachmanides this is the view also taken in Talmud J. which he cites in his comment on Lev. 14, 4. See also Rashi Deut. 22, 6, where he adopts the view that צפור includes unclean birds.

view, (viz. that Halakah is the product of Midrashic exegesis), points rather to the contrary. The following example will help to illustrate: The words in Lev. 19, 26: "Ye shall not eat anything with the blood", are variously interpreted in Halakah as (1) a prohibition against eating the flesh of the sacrifices before the blood has been sprinkled;[37] (2) a prohibition against eating flesh from an animal whose blood is still in it, i.e., whose life has not yet departed;[38] (3) a prohibition against members of a Court eating any food on the day of the execution of a decree of capital punishment pronounced by that Court.[39] What a remarkable diversity of laws associated with a few Biblical words! If the Rabbis were merely concerned with the plain meaning of the text and from these various interpretations, one interpretation embodying one of the laws—and one only—had been accepted, there would be some point in Rosenblatt's argument.[40] But such is not the case; all these Halakoth were accepted as binding. Their very diversity, and the many interpretations on which they are based, show that the Rabbis do not purport to give the plain meaning of the text, but are merely employing it for the purpose of deriving from Scripture some kind of 'support' for the Halakoth. In the light of this we are able to understand the Rabbinic statement:

---

37 Sanh. 63a. ......

38 Sanh. ibid.

39 Sanh. ibid. And for an even more fanciful interpretation on this text see Ber. 10b.

40 S. Rosenblatt, 'Bible Interpretation in the Mishnah', Baltimore, 1935, p. 5.

מקרא אחד יוצא לכמה טעמים "One Biblical verse may convey several teachings".[41]

As to the third argument, it should be pointed out that it was only when new questions and problems arose, not dealt with in detail by the traditional Halakoth, that the Rabbis sought to derive the solution for their Halakic decisions from Scriptural exegesis.[42] In such cases—relatively few in number—we do find that "two divergent views derive their authority from the same source" and admittedly, in such cases "the Halakah was the result of the exegesis". But these Halakoth follow fairly closely the correct meaning of the context and do not support the view that the Rabbis did not understand the natural sense of Scripture.

Reverting to the 'traditional' Halakoth, it cannot be sufficiently emphasised that the Scriptural sources cited are not necessarily intended to represent the plain meaning of the text.[43] In this connection the following passages from the Mishnah, Babylonian and Jerusalem Talmuds respectively, are of considerable interest.[44]

1. *Mishnah In Ḥag.* 10a: "(The laws concerning) the dissolution of vows hover in the air and have nought to

---

41 Sanh. 34a. It should be noted that it is the 'School of R. Ishmael', the follower of Peshaṭ, that is responsible for this statement. Cf. the Rabbinic principle אין מקרא יוצא מידי פשוטו discussed infra pp. 73-4.

42 E.g. Mishnah T'rumah, 6, 6. Cf. I. Halevy, 'Doroth ha-Rishonim', Frankfurt a.M., 1918, vol. 1e, pp. 467-522.

43 Cf. infra pp. 66-9.

44 See N. Krochmal, 'Moreh Nebuke ha-Zeman', Lemberg, 1863, Shaar 13; and I. Halevy, 'Doroth ha-Rishonim,' vol. 1e pp. 467-522.

rest on.[45] The laws concerning the Sabbath, festal-offerings, acts of trespass, are as mountains hanging by a hair, for they have scant Scriptural basis, but many laws, (the laws concerning) civil cases and (Temple) services, Levitical cleanness and uncleanness, and the forbidden relations have what to rest on, and it is they[46] that are the essentials of the Torah".

2. *Moed Ḳaṭan* 5a: "R. Simeon b. Pazzi said: Where is an indication in the Torah that gravesides should be marked? In the instructive text: '(And when they pass through . . . the land) and one seeth a man's bone then shall he set up a sign by it'.[47] Said Rabina to R. Ashi, 'But who told us that before Ezekiel came?'[48] (Said the other): 'Accepting your view, with regard to the statement made by R. Ḥisda[49] (namely): 'This point we do not learn from the law of our Master Moses; we learn it from the words of (prophet) Ezekiel the son of Buzi . . . (we might equally ask), who had told us that before Ezekiel came and stated it? Only, that was first learnt by oral tradition and then Ezekiel came and gave us a textual basis for it; here too, it was first learnt as an oral tradition and then Ezekiel came and gave us a textual basis for it'."

---

45 I.e., in Biblical teaching, and depend only on oral tradition, Rashi.

46 "These and those are essentials of the Torah", according to the Gemara 1.c. 11b.

47 Ezek. 39, 15.

48 I.e., where is it intimated in the Pentateuch, the main source of Law?

49 Zeb. 22b. in reference to another law.

3. *Jerushalmi Berakoth* 2, 3: "Whenever a proposition is not evident, they (the Rabbis) try to support it by a large number of Biblical passages".

In many cases the Biblical verse is adduced merely as a 'mnemonic'. As the traditional teaching was preserved without the aid of writing,[50] it would have required a prodigious memory to retain all the doctrines and ideas, Halakic as well as Haggadic, which were handed down from generation to generation. The practice of associating a traditional Halakah with a Biblical verse was due partly to a desire to assist the memory.

Both in the Talmud and Midrashim we frequently find the Rabbis employing various kinds of mnemonical devices.[51] In Erub. 54b they are expressly referred to; thus: "The Torah can only be acquired with (the aid of) mnemonic signs, for it is said, 'Put it in their mouth';[52] read not 'put it' (שימה) but 'its mnemonic sign' (סימנה). R. Taḥlifa of the West heard this and proceeding to R. Abbahu told it to him. You, the other said to him, deduced this from that text; we deduce it from this one: 'Set thee up way-marks, make thee' etc.;[53] devise mnemonic signs for the Torah". Scriptural passages, in particular, were used[54] to assist in the teaching of Torah; as

50 See Giṭ. 60b; Tem. 14b; J. Meg. 4, 1. Cf. also N. Krochmal, 'Moreh Nebuke ha-Zeman', Shaar 13.

51 E.g. Shab. 60b, 66a and 96a; Taan. 10a; Yeb. 21a; Ḥul. 62b; Eruk. 11a; Nid. 45b, a.e.

52 Deut. 31, 19.

53 Jer. 31, 21.

54 E.g. Shab. 90b; Keth. 72b; B. Meẓ. 86a and 117a; Ab. Zarah 8a, 9a, 9b, 29a, 39a; Nid. 45b, a.e.

a rule, the pupils were thoroughly versed in the contents of the entire Scripture.[55] Indeed, we occasionally find a Rabbi stating quite frankly that a Biblical word, phrase or verse is not cited as a 'proof' (ראיה) but merely as a suggestion or 'reminder'[56] (זכר) of the Halakah, or as an 'allusion'[57] (רמז). In some cases, a Biblical text is expressed to be adduced as an אסמכתא 'support' which is intended to add some degree of authority to the particular Halakah, but the Halakic interpretation is not taken by the Rabbis to represent the meaning of the text. It is in this sense that we have to understand the Rabbis' rhetorical question: מי איכא מלתא בכתובי דלא רמזה משה באורייתא "Is it possible that there is something in the Hagiographa to which Moses did not allude in the Pentateuch?"[58]

An interesting illustration is to be seen in Ḥul. 27a, which deals with the ritual concerning the slaughter of animals (שחיטה). In this passage a Biblical text is sought for the traditional ritual—viz. שחיטה מן הצואר ("slaughter through the throat"), which is not referred to either in Scripture or in the Mishnah. Various texts are suggested by Tannaim as well as Amoraim, but the conclusion arrived at is that the ritual is mere "tradition".[59] Accordingly, the texts quoted by the Rabbis in connection with this traditional ritual are not intended by them to serve

55 Cf. infra pp. 83-5, 91-4.

56 E. g. Mishnah Shab. 8, 7, and 9, 4.

57 E. g. Meg. 2a; M. Ḳaṭan 5a; Sanh. 81b, a.e.

58 Taan. 9a.

59 Ḥul. 27a. See very important statement in Tosafoth B. Bathra 147a. s.v. מניין.

as a basis for it, but are merely drawn into association with it. In the bulk of the Rabbinic exegesis it is not the ordinary meaning of the text which they purport to expound, but rather an artificial meaning which seeks to deduce support for laws already in force, for the expansion of such laws, or the introduction of others. Moreover, it is not unlikely that the rise of the Sadducean movement gave an added impetus to this aspect of Rabbinic exegesis. As G. H. Box remarks: "The Sadducees questioned the legitimacy of the traditional laws on the ground that they could not be proved from the letter of the law, it was necessary therefore that a systematic attempt should be made to deduce the laws from the Scriptural text. Hence the production of Halakic Midrashim".[60]

As a further illustration, of the manner in which the Biblical text was employed by the Rabbis to serve as a mnemonic, may be cited the very frequent[61] use in the Talmud and Midrash of the formula אל תקרי "Read not thus, but thus", already referred to.[62] Some scholars, quite erroneously, consider that where this formula is found the Rabbis seriously intended the variant reading and suggested interpretations to be taken as the actual meaning of the text.[63] This view has been stated by F. W.

---

60 G. H. Box, introduction to 'Sifre on Numbers', by Levertoff, London, 1926. Cf. I. H. Weiss, 'Dor', vol. 1, ch. 18; J.E. vol. 8, p. 549; R. T. Herford, 'Pharisees', ch. 3.

61 About one hundred and ten times.

62 Supra p. 66.

63 E. g. E. Levita, introduction to his 'Massoreth Ha-Massoreth'; A. W. Streane, General Index s.v. "Readings", in his translation of Ḥagigah, Cambridge, 1891.

Farrar, who says: "The אל תקרי is an absolutely arbitrary device for making the Scriptures say exactly what the interpreter wished to make them say. Thus the Bible was forced to imply thousands of things of which the writers never dreamed . . . hence the incessant Rabbinic formula 'Read not so, but so' ".[64]

That the Rabbis did not intend their suggested variations and interpretations as the plain meaning can be seen from many examples. Here is one.[65]

In Keth. 5a we find: "Bar-Ḳappara expounded: What is the meaning of what is written, 'And thou shalt have a peg among thy implements?'[66] Do not read 'thy implements'[67] but 'upon thine ear';[68] this means to say that if a man hears an unworthy thing he shall plug his finger[69] into his ears". It can hardly be imagined that the Rabbis were ignorant of the plain meaning of this simple verse.[70]

The real purpose of the formula has been well expressed by C. Taylor, thus: "The exegetical device 'Read not so, but so' is often used in the Talmud when it is desired to attach a preconceived idea to a Scriptural expression by way of *μνημόσυνον*. The אל תקרי is not to be taken as evidence that an actual variant reading was current:

---

64 F. W. Farrar, 'History of Interpretation', London, 1886, p. 104.
65 From Maimonides, 'Guide', part 3, ch. 43.
66 Deut. 23, 14.
67 From אָזֵן 'implement', 'tool'.
68 As if from אֹזֶן 'ear'.
69 The finger is pointed like a peg.
70 In fact this text is literally understood in Yoma 75b.

on the contrary, the words to which it is prefixed are confessedly the true reading, with which the Darshan makes free for a special purpose".[71] In support of this view it is significant to note that the same interpretation is frequently introduced in one instance by the formula and in another without the formula, and at times the interpretations, both with and without the formula are attributed to the same author.[72]

Haggadah, unlike Halakah, is characterised by a much freer handling of the text, since it was not conditioned by certain defined hermeneutical principles, though we do find the same kind of expressions used in citing Scriptures, e.g., מניין (whence . . . ?), דכתיב (as it

---

71 C. Taylor, 'Sayings of the Jewish Fathers', Cambridge, 1877, 6, 3 note 2. With reference to this formula cf. I. D. Bamberger, introduction to 'Ḳoreh Be-Emeth', Frankfurt a.M., 1871; B. Epstein, introduction to 'Maḳḳor Baruk', Wilna, 1928, ch. 9; Maimonides, 'Guide', part 3, ch. 43; RaSHBA on B. Bathra, p. 78; של"ה, Jozefov, 1878, essay, 'Torah She-Be'al Peh', p. 40; P. E. Hurwitz, 'Sefer ha-Berith', Warsaw, 1889, part 2, section 12 ch. 5; I. B. Levinsohn, 'Te'uddah Beyisroel', Warsaw, 1878, ch. 3 note 1; Introduction to 'Eẓ Joseph', in 'En Jacob', Wilna; Z. H. Chajes, 'Introduction to the Talmud', Zolkiev, 1845, ch. 17; M. Friedlander, 'Jewish Religion', 7th ed., London, 1937, p. 204; J. Emden, on Eruk. 15b; M. Gudeman in 'Jewish Quarterly Review', O.S. vol. 4, p. 348; J. Scott Porter, 'Principles of Textual Criticism', London, 1848, p. 50; and the 'Journal of Theological Studies', London, 1900, vol. 1, p. 407, note 1.

72 E. g. Ber. 30b with formula and J. Ber. 5, 1 without formula; Ber. 48b with formula, J. Ber. 7, 1 without formula; Shab. 89a with formula, Gen. R. 18, 6 without formula; Erub. 19a with formula, Ber. 57a and Sanh. 37a without formula; Erub. 54a with formula, Deut. R. 8, 4 without formula; Meg. 28a with formula, B. Ḳamma 93a without formula; Men. 29b with formula, J. Ḥag. 2, 1 without formula.

is written).[73] Moreover, in the Haggadah the imagination had freer play, Halakah being concerned with logical argument and reasoning. Interpretations in the Haggadah are at times so fanciful that they could not possibly have been intended as serious expositions of the Biblical text.

The fallacy underlying the opinions of some scholars lies in their failure to distinguish between the two elements of Rabbinic exegesis, the prevalent Midrashic exegesis (not intended to represent the plain meaning), and the ordinary exegesis (directed to the plain meaning of the text). The following two examples will serve to bring out this distinction:

(a) Is. 1, 17: אַשְּׁרוּ חמוץ "Relieve the oppressed". Raba[74] interprets the verse artificially to mean: אשרי דיין שמחמץ את דינו "Praise the judge who reserves his verdict", (i.e., by interpreting חמוץ from חָמֵץ, 'sour', in the sense of preserving, and hence metaphorically 'to postpone', to keep in 'reserve'). It is important to bear in mind that Raba, the author of this interpretation, in another passage[75] states the established rule אין מקרא יוצא מידי פשוטו

73 Even popular sayings of the age are occasionally associated with a Biblical text; see e. g. Sanh. 7b, B. Ḳamma 92a and b and in many other places. Cf. Eẓ Joseph in the introduction to 'En Jacob', Wilna.

74 Sanh. 35a.

75 Yeb. 24a. Cf. infra p. 77.

"A Biblical verse can never lose its literal sense".[76] Raba's point in citing the verse (Is. 1, 17) is only for the purpose of emphasising that a judge should carefully consider his judgment; he does not pretend to give the plain meaning. This is clear from another reference by Raba to the same verse (as recorded in Yoma 39b and Ḳid. 35a) where he explains the word חמצן ("a grasping person") on the analogy of the use of חמוץ ("oppressed") in the verse.

(b) Deut. 24, 16: לא יומתו אבות על בנים ובנים לא יומתו על אבות "The fathers shall not be put to death for (על) the children, neither shall the children be put to death for the fathers". The plain meaning of the verse is that the family of a criminal is not to be punished for his crime. In Sanh. 27b however, we find a Rabbinic interpretation which expounds the word על in the sense of "through" or "on account of" i.e., "by the testimony" of the members of his family. The passage in Deut. is in fact referred to twice in the Bible itself[77] and in each case the context is set out in its simple and natural sense. In the circumstances, it is most unlikely that the Rabbinic interpreter was unaware of the plain meaning of the verse. Actually, in another Talmudic passage,[78] the verse is cited in its plain meaning; likewise in Ber. 7a, where

---

76 To be distinguished from the expression פשטא דקרא. The latter is rendered by M. Jastrow, s.v. פשטא, 'Plain sense (not homiletically forced)', though occasionally the expression is used to introduce an interpretation which does not necessarily accord with the plain or literal meaning. Cf. Erub. 23b; Ḳid. 80b; Ḥul. 6a and 133a.

77 2 Kings 14, 6; 2 Chron. 25, 4.

78 Yeb. 79a.

the plain meaning is indicated and sought to be reconciled with the apparently-contradictory text in Ex. 34, 7.

Reference has already been made[79] to the Rabbinic statement: אין מקרא יוצא מידי פשוטו "A Biblical verse can never lose its literal sense" (although its meaning may be extended by the methods of interpretation).[80] This statement is to be found only in three passages (Shab. 63a, Yeb. 11b and Yeb. 24a) but the principle involved is fundamental in Rabbinic exegesis.[81] I. H. Weiss[82] and L. Zweifel,[83] consistently with their views on Rabbinic exegesis, regard the statement as a categorical assertion by the Rabbis that their interpretations—however fanciful they may appear to us—never deviated from Peshaṭ,[84] and accordingly, they conclude that the Rabbis did not understand the plain meaning. F. W. Farrar, in similar vein, states: "Some of the Soferim had laid down the rule that every interpretation was to accord with the literal (אין מקרא יוצא מידי פשוטו), but no one practically attended to it."[85] These critics are mistaken, for, as we shall see,

---

79 Supra p. 71.

80 Translation from M. Jastrow s.v. מקרא.

81 Cf. Ibn Ezra, introduction to his Commentary on Daniel (quoted in 'Essays on Ibn Ezra', by M. Friedlander, London, 1877, p. 96); and in his introduction to his Commentary on Pent., Method 4. See infra notes 86-7.

82 'Dor', vol. 1, ch. 18; cf. also his contribution in 'Kokebe Yiẓḥaḳ', by M. Stern, No. 37, where he again misinterprets this principle.

83 L. Zweifel, 'Sanegor', Warsaw, 1885, p. 147.

84 I. H. Weiss has been strongly criticised on this point in 'Hashiloaḥ', vol. 7, Jan.-June, 1901, p. 209, note 2.

85 F. W. Farrar, 'History of Interpretation', London 1886, p. 95, note 2.

the true meaning of the principle involved, accepted and understood in Rabbinic literature, is that Midrashic exegesis cannot annul the primary sense of the text.[86]

It is significant to observe that in the three Talmudic passages referred to, the principle under consideration is stated not as one enunciated for the first time, but as a principle universally recognised and authoritatively accepted as binding.[87] Its origin can be traced back to the time when, with the extensive development of Midrashic interpretation and the gradual submerging of plain exegesis, it became necessary to counteract, to some

---

86 Cf. Rashi, Yeb. 24a s.v. אין מקרא; Suk. 2a s.v. למען ידעו and in his introduction to the commentary on Canticles; Maimonides, 'Sefer Hamitzvoth', Shoresh 2; 'Tosafoth' on Yoma 62b s.v. מוספין; Ibn Ezra, 'Introduction' to his commentary on Pent. Method 4, and his introduction to Daniel (quoted in 'Essays on Ibn Ezra' by M. Friedlander, London, 1877, p. 96 note 2); Dei Rossi, 'Meor Enayim', Vienna, 1829, essay 'Imre Binah', ch. 15; M. Ḥagiz, 'Eleh ha-Mitẓvoth', Wandsbeck, 1713, commenting on Levirate marriage; M. Mendelsohn, 'Introduction' to Pent.; I. B. Levinsohn, 'Te'uddah Be'Yisroel', Warsaw, 1878, ch. 5, note 2; N. Krochmal, 'Moreh Nebuke ha-Zeman', Lemberg, 1863, ch. 14; M. Landau, Introduction to 'Pithron Hamiloth', Prague, 1827; 'Tosefoth Yom-Ṭob', on Yeb. 2, 8; Z. Frankel, 'Darke ha-Mishnah', Warsaw, 1923, ch. 1; Z. H. Chajes, 'Introduction to the Talmud', Zolkiev, 1845, ch. 17; S. D. Luzzatto, (quoted in 'Sanegor' by L. Zweifel, p. 149); P. E. Hurwitz, 'Sefer ha-Berith', Warsaw, 1889, part 2, sect. 12, ch. 5; K. Perlo, 'Oẓar Lashon Ḥaḥamim', s.v. אין מקרא; J. Jolles, 'Melo Haronim', part 3, s.v. ו' קטועה; 'Hashiloaḥ' vol. 7, Jan.-June, 1901, p. 209, note 2.

87 Cf. Ibn Ezra on Ex. 13, 9; Z. H. Chajes, 'Introduction to the Talmud', ch. 17; for a contrary view see W. Bacher, J.E., vol. 3, p. 165. E. Deutsch, in his Essay 'The Talmud', p. 14 refers to this principle as "the primary exegetical law of the Talmud".

extent, the new exegesis. While extending Midrashic interpretation even to the length of deviating from the literal meaning of the text, the Rabbis had to ensure at the same time that the Midrashic exegesis should not be confused with Peshaṭ.[88] The principle demonstrates the Rabbis' keen awareness of the distinction between Peshaṭ and Drash. Let us now examine the three passages.

1. Shab. 63a: The Rabbis, taking the plain meaning of Ps. 45, 4, "Gird thy sword upon thy thigh, O mighty one, Thy glory and thy majesty", refer to it as showing that a "sword" is commonly regarded as an article of personal adornment.[89] R. Kahana rejects this in favour of a current Midrashic interpretation whereby the text is taken as referring to the study of the Torah, and here Mar b. D'ravina calls his attention to the principle.

It is to be observed, on the one hand, that Mar b. D'ravina does not question the Midrashic interpretation as such; on the other hand, he emphasises that the word חרב in the text, as ordinarily interpreted, can only mean "sword". In other words, while accepting the Midrashic interpretation for the purpose of edification, he insists that in ascertaining the meaning of a word in a particular text the primary sense of the text must be considered, contending that the Midrashic treatment must be regarded as such, but without affecting the primary meaning, which no form of exegesis can annul. R. Kahana's confession that, although he knew the whole of the Talmud by the time he was eighteen, he only became aware of

---

88 Cf. I. B. Levinsohn, 'Beth Yehudah', ch. 114, note 2; R. T. Herford, 'Pharisees', ch. 3.

89 I. e. may therefore be carried on the Sabbath.

this principle years later, need not be taken as an indication of the general standard of Bible study in his day.[90] For, as S. Horowitz[91] remarks, "R. Kahana wishes to stress the fact that he was an exception to the rule".[92]

2. Yeb. 11b: This passage relates to the prohibition in Deut. 24, 4, against the husband re-marrying his divorced wife who had been married again. According to the plain meaning of the text, the prohibition takes effect on the termination of the second marriage, whether by the death of the second husband or by divorce. As far as the first husband is concerned, the wife is regarded as "unclean" (טמאה), since she had had marital relations with another man. This plain interpretation is given by R. Jose in the name of R. Eliezer. The Ḥaḥamim, however, relate the word הטמאה[93] ("defiled") to a סוטה (a wife of proven infidelity).[94] In this connection, a Rabbi of a later generation queried whether the Ḥaḥamim intended to apply the term הטמאה only to a סוטה, in which case they would be disregarding the rule,[95] or whether they gave it a more extensive meaning (adding the class of סוטה to that of מחזיר גרושתו), thereby keeping themselves within the limit of the principle.

90 As understood by W. Bacher, J.E., vol. 3, p. 165.

91 J.E., vol. 8, p. 548.

92 Z. H. Chajes in his 'Introduction to the Talmud', Zolkiev, 1845, ch. 17, takes the view that R. Kahana is referring only to texts of a poetical nature (like the text under treatment).

93 Of that particular text.

94 Rejecting the application of the term 'defiled' to the divorced wife, since her relations with her second husband had been legalised by marriage.

95 That "a Biblical verse can never lose its literal sense".

3. Yeb. 24a: With reference to the Rabbinic interpretation of Deut. 25, 6, Raba observes: "although the principle that a Biblical verse can never lose its literal sense applies to the 'whole Torah', yet in this particular case the Peshaṭ is annulled 'entirely' ". The importance of Raba's statement is twofold; it conveys the idea firstly, that the principle applies to the whole Torah, and secondly, by inference, that while some latitude must be accorded to Halakic exegesis, the primary meaning, as a general rule, must not be lost sight of "entirely".[96]

In Haggadah, much more frequently than in Halakah, the Biblical text is treated very freely, in some instances to a degree of extreme licence. But although the Haggadah had acquired considerable importance, its interpretations were not intended to represent the plain meaning of the text. An interesting legend in J. Sanh. 10, 2 relates that R. Levi lectured for six months on 1 Kings 21, 25, elaborating on Ahab's wickedness. Ahab appeared to him in a dream and remonstrated with him, and as a result, during the following six months, the Rabbi spoke as Ahab's defender, still using the same verse, but with the omission of the middle clause. The implication of the legend is quite clear, viz. that the author is merely 'expounding' the text (i.e., homiletically) rather than interpreting it. Indeed, as the following examples will show, in some passages the Rabbis themselves expressly distinguish between homiletical exposition and plain interpretation.

---

96 See Rashi 1. c. and N. Krochmal, 'Moreh Nebuke ha-Zeman', Lemberg, 1877, ch. 14.

(a) Taanith 5b: R. Isaac quotes R. Joḥanan as stating that "our Father Jacob did not die", whereupon R. Naḥman questions him: 'Was it for nought that the embalmers embalmed and wailers wailed?', to which R. Isaac replies: 'Thus said R. Joḥanan, I am only *expounding* a verse' ".

(b) Giṭ. 7a: When R. Huna begins his discourse on the words "Kinah and Dimunah and Ad'addah"[97] R. Ashi observes that the text merely speaks of the settlements of the land of Israel, whereupon R. Huna exclaims: "Do I not know myself that it speaks of settlements of the land of Israel?—but R. G'biha gave the following exposition".

In Haggadah, to such an extent was the meaning of the text strained that we occasionally find some Rabbis protesting. Thus R. Ishmael, in repudiating an Haggadic interpretation of Eliezer b. Hyrkanos, remarks: "Truly you say to Scripture, 'Be silent while I am expounding' ".[98] Again, R. Jose remarks, with reference to an Haggadic interpretation of the word חדרך in Zech. 9, 1: "How much longer will you pervert the meaning of Scripture? I call heaven and earth to testify that I am from Damascus and nearby is a place called Hadrach".[99] In similar vein, R. Tarfon, in dealing with a curious Haggadic statement of R. Eliezer, says: "How long will you rake words?"[100] Actually, R. Eliezer makes it quite

97 Josh. 15, 22.

98 Sifra on Lev. 13, 47.

99 Sifre on Deut. 1, 1; Jalḳuṭ on Zech. §575.

100 Yoma 76a.

clear in his reply that he is not really interpreting the verse "I am only getting intimation in a Bible verse".

Perhaps the most interesting example of all occurs in Midrash Gen. R. 80, 1, where we are told that R. Judah was incensed at an interpretation given by R. Jose of Onaah in relation to Hos. 5, 6. R. Lakish succeeded in appeasing him with the following argument: "If we think well of those Gentiles who introduce a mime in the theatre and circus performance with a view to preventing idle chattering and quarrelling, (how much more so should we think well of R. Jose), yet you rail at one who is well versed in Torah". This incident, is important not only because it shows a tendency by some of the Rabbinic scholars to decry the licence taken in Midrashic exegesis, but also because of the argument used by R. Lakish, which suggests that this extreme form of exegesis may occasionally have served as a kind of light relief or entertainment, though of an edifying character.

Notwithstanding the manifest divergence between many of the Rabbinic interpretations and the ordinary meaning of the Biblical text, scholars such as J. H. Mecklenburg[101] and Malbim[102] not only held that they were presented as serious exegesis, but actually accepted them as such. On the other hand, H. Graetz, I. H. Weiss, F. W. Farrar and their followers, while regarding such interpretations as seriously intended, took the equally-extreme view that the Rabbis failed to understand the plain meaning of the text. The premise on which this conclusion is based has been shown to be false.

---

101 In his 'Ha-Ketab weha-Ḳabbalah'.

102 In his commentaries on the Bible, Mekilta, Sifra and Sifre.

The deviation in Rabbinic exegesis from the path of plain interpretation does not warrant a conclusion that the ancient Rabbis had not a keen appreciation of Peshaṭ. There can be no doubt that the Rabbis had a fluent and intimate knowledge of Scripture in all its facets. It is not as though the Rabbis "strayed further and further away from a natural and commonsense interpretation",[103] but rather that Peshaṭ was not the main field of their research. The simple interpretation of the Bible was not their main task. That task devolved on the elementary school-teachers who instructed the young. The knowledge of Scripture in its ordinary meaning was an indispensable part of the education of the Rabbinic scholar, but it constituted his primary education only. His advanced education consisted in the Studies of the vast store of traditional exposition and interpretation. "But although Rabbinic literature does not purport to deal with plain exegesis, there is to be found throughout its numerous tomes a wealth of objective exegetical material which still remains to be sifted".[104] It is hoped in the following chapters to afford further and more positive evidence of these aspects of Rabbinic exegesis.

---

103 J.E., vol. 3, p. 165.

104 From an unpublished work by J. Baker. Cf. infra p. 105.

CHAPTER FOUR

CHAPTER FOUR

THE RABBIS AND THE STUDY OF THE BIBLE

From what has been indicated in the preceding chapter, no serious objection can be taken to W. R. Smith's statement that "their (the Soferim's) real interest lay ... not in the sacred text itself, but in the practical system based upon it". But he is quite mistaken when he refers to the study of Scripture as being "spoken of (by the Rabbis) almost contemptuously as something far inferior to the study of the traditional legislative system".[1] Undoubtedly, the study of the Bible in itself was not intended as a complete course for the Rabbinic scholar; in this sense it was but a means to an end. At the same time, the knowledge of Scripture as a subject was always regarded by the Rabbis as of great importance; it was an essential prerequisite in the training of the Rabbinic scholar. According to a passage in Ḳid. 30a, the command: "And ye shall teach them your children"[2] is fulfilled by teaching of Bible only.[3]

---

1 W. R. Smith, 'Old Testament in the Jewish Church', London, 1895, 2nd ed., p. 52. "It has not infrequently been asserted that the Jews regarded it (the Talmud) as superior in authority to the Scriptures, but, as will be seen, such is not the case", 'The Talmud', by D. Wright, London, 1932, p. 20.

2 Deut. 11, 19.

3 Cf. J. H. Hertz ad loc.

The "investigation" of Scripture formed the life's work of the Rabbis, and their remarkable acquaintance with the whole of the Bible is evidenced throughout the Talmud and Midrashim. "A striking instance may be seen in the Mekilta, a small work of not more than seventy octavo pages when stripped from its commentaries; it has about one thousand citations from the Prophets and the Hagiographa".[4]

The Rabbis emphasised repeatedly that "a scholar (a תלמיד חכם) ought to be thoroughly versed in the twenty-four Books, and if he lacks the knowledge of even one of them he is not a scholar".[5] Indeed, for a scholar, ignorance of a Biblical verse was a mark of discredit.[6] In Song R. 5, 13 we are told that a scholar "ought to be filled with a knowledge of Scripture, Mishnah, Talmud, Halakoth and Haggadoth". It is significant that in all references by the Rabbis to the component parts of Torah or to the order in which these subjects should be taught, the study of Scripture comes first. In the Mishnah[7] we are told: "Five years (is the age) for (the study of) Scripture, ten for (the study of) Mishnah, fifteen for (the study of) Talmud", from which it is seen that five years was to be devoted to the study of Scripture. The same idea of the priority of Scripture, found in several other Rabbinic

---

4 S. Schechter, 'Some Aspects of Rabbinic Theology', N.Y., 1909, p. 122; see also J.E., vol. 12, pp. 196-197. In Meg. 18b, we are told that R. Ḥananneel was able to write the whole Torah from memory.

5 Song R. 4, 11; cf. Ex. R. 41, 5.

6 Shab. 152b.

7 Aboth, 5, 24.

passages,[8] is beautifully expressed in the Haggadic statement: "When the Holy One, blessed be He, revealed Himself on Sinai to give the Torah unto Israel, He said it unto Moses in the following order: Scripture, Mishnah, Talmud and Haggadah".[9] To the Rabbis it was inconceivable that the higher studies could be undertaken without a thorough grounding in Scripture. The Rabbis say:[10] "The fool enters the Synagogue, and seeing there people occupying themselves with the law he asks: 'How does a man begin to learn the law?' They answer him; 'First a man reads from a scroll, then the Book (of the law), and then the Prophets, and then the Hagiographa: when he has completed the study of the Scriptures he learns the Talmud, and then the Halakoth, and then the Haggadoth' ".

Not every student completed the full course of Rabbinic learning. The Rabbis commented: "It is a common experience that out of a thousand people that enter upon the study of the Bible, a hundred succeed; while out of that hundred entering upon the study of the Mishnah, only ten succeed; and out of those ten that enter on the study of the Talmud, only one succeeds".[11] It is from this select minority that Rabbinic literature came. The vast majority did not get beyond "the study of the Bible", which, in contrast with the main contents of Rabbinic

---

8 Gen. R. 66, 3; Lev. R. 15, 2; Erub. 21b; Suk. 28a; Meg. 28b; Ḳid. 30a; Keth. 50a and 103b; B. Bathra 134a; Sifre on Deut. 32, 2, a. e.

9 Ex. R. 47, 1.

10 Deut. R. 8, 3.

11 Lev. R. 2, 1; Ḳoheleth R. 7, 28.

literature, can only mean simple instruction in the plain meaning of Scripture. Such instruction, as will be shown later, commenced in the primary schools for children.

It was encumbent upon the Jew to study the Bible continually. The scholar who has already acquired a knowledge of Bible, Mishnah and Talmud is enjoined by the Rabbis to devote a third of every day, for the rest of his life, to the study of Bible.[12] Thorough knowledge and deep understanding of Scripture was demanded by the Rabbis. "Restrain your children from recitation",[13] R. Eliezer advised his disciples from his sick-bed.[14] Moreover, besides hearing the recital of the weekly lection from the Pentateuch and Prophets in the Synagogue, it was recommended that the Sidrah of the week be read through at home, twice in the original and once in the Aramaic translation, the Targum.[15] Rabbenu Haḳadosh, in his verbal testament, commanded his sons not to eat on the Sabbath until the weekly Sidrah had been read through.[16] The fact that the Targum on the Pentateuch was likewise read in the Synagogue and at home is also of importance when one remembers that on the whole the Targum is a faithful translation and explains many difficult passages.

From various passages in the Talmud it is clear that the Rabbis required the public translator, known as the

---

12 Ḳid. 30a; Ab. Zarah 19b.

13 "Parading a superficial knowledge of the Bible by verbal memorising", Jastrow s.v. הגיון.

14 Ber. 28b.

15 Ber. 8a.

16 Cf. Tosafoth Ber. 8b s.v. ישלים.

'Meturgeman' (Aramaic for 'Interpreter or Translator') to translate the Scripture in accordance with the plain meaning of the text. Occasionally they condemn a periphrastic rendering, e.g., in Mishnah Meg. 4, 9, we find: "He who renders periphrastically portions concerning incest, we silence him"; i.e., the rendering of קלון (disgrace) for ערוה (nakedness) is prohibited. Authorities[17] consider that the prohibition in this Mishnah is not confined to Lev., chapters 18 and 20, but refers to all Biblical passages dealing with sexual immorality. The same Mishnah contains another interesting prohibition against the deviation by the Meturgeman from the plain meaning: "He who translates 'And thou shalt not give any of thy seed to set them apart to Molech' by 'And thou shalt not give any of thy seed (to a heathen woman) to become with child in idolatry', we silence him with a sharp rebuke".

It is important to note, in this connection, that contrary to the express prohibition in the Mishnah, we find recorded in the Talmud[18] that R. Joseph renders ערוה by קלון (disgrace) and that Targ. Jon. as well as the school of R. Ishmael, interpret Lev. 18, 21 in the manner specifically prohibited.[19] But there is really no inconsistency, since the Mishnah refers only to the renderings by the public translator; it is significant that Targ. Onḳ., which is the authorized translation, renders Lev. 18, 21 in accordance with the Mishnah. Indeed, because of the contrary

17 Cf. J. Rabinowitz, 'Mishnah Meg.', 4, 9, London, 1931, p. 132.

18 Meg. 25a.

19 See Meg. 25a. Rashi's explanation l.c. does not bear a critical examination.

interpretation mentioned in the Talmudic source, the Mishnah referred to has an added bearing on our subject. It shows the clear distinction between the teaching of Bible as such and its exposition for the purpose of exegesis. The institution of the Meturgeman arose in order that the general public, whose vernacular was Aramaic, might become acquainted with the original text of Scripture. The translator was required to present the plain meaning only, free renderings being discouraged. But among advanced scholars, who would already be acquainted with the original text of Scripture and its ordinary interpretation, it would be quite in accordance with traditional practice to "search" the text for some deeper meaning.[20]

To ensure that the Bible was presented to the public in its plain meaning, the Rabbis gave specific instructions to the Meturgeman regarding the form and substance of his rendering. For example: "If one translates a verse literally, he is a liar; if he adds thereto, he is a blasphemer and a libeller".[21] In the case of obscene or indelicate words the Mishnah[22] — more elaborately so the Gemara[23] — specifies those which may be read in the Synagogue and translated, and others which may be read but not translated.

---

20 See 'Tosefoth Yom-Ṭob'; 'Tifereth Yisrael', and Z. H. Chajes on Meg. 4, 9.

21 Ḳid. 49a; Tosefta Ḳid. ch. 3. This refers to the public translations in the Synagogue alongside the reading of the Law, which was also a feature of ancient times.

22 Meg. 4, 10.

23 Meg. 25b.

An interesting passage occurs in the Talmud[24] דברים שבכתב אי אתה רשאי לאומרן על פה דברים שבעל פה אי אתה רשאי לאומרן בכתב "Written matter (Biblical passages) must not be recited from memory, and verbally-transmitted words must not be recited from writing". Such regulations were in all likelihood prompted by a desire for the preservation of Peshaṭ, by avoiding the possibility of orally-transmitted interpretations obtaining the authority attaching to that which has received permanent form in writing.[25]

In view of the importance placed by Rabbinic Judaism on the study of Scripture, it is not surprising to find that children were instructed in it from early childhood.[26] Aboth 5, 24 states: "At five years the age is reached for the study of Scripture". In B. Bathra 21a we find Rab giving R. Samuel b. Shilath (an elementary teacher)[27] the following direction: "Until six years of age take no pupils, from six and upwards take (the child) and feed him (with knowledge) as you feed an ox".[28] In Keth. 50a this direction is held to refer only to the teaching of Scripture, not to the more advanced studies. The teaching of Scripture was the main function of the "Beth-Sefer" (primary school); "the Beth-Sefer", we are told, "was the school

---

24 Giṭ. 60b.

25 Cf. S. Rosenfield, 'Mishpaḥath Soferim', Wilna, 1883, p. 6, § 3. See also C. D. Ginsburg, in his article 'Scribes' 1, 3, in Kitto's 'Cyclopædia of Biblical Literature', Edinburgh, 3rd ed.

26 "Philo and Josephus point with pride to the fact that Jewish children, from early childhood, were instructed in the 'Law' and the tradition of their fathers", J.E., vol. 5, s.v. 'Education'.

27 B. Bathra 8b.

28 Translation from Jastrow s.v. ספי.

for Bible"—(בית ספר למקרא).[29] Many other references to the teaching of Bible, and to Bible-teachers, are to be found in Rabbinic literature.[30]

The Talmud records random accounts of conversations with young children about their Bible lessons. It appears to have been a common practice to address to "a young child" (ינוקא) the familiar words: פסוק לי פסוקך "Tell me thy verse",[31] i.e., to ask him to recite the verse he had learned that day in his Bible lesson. Two instances are especially noteworthy, one mentioned in Taanith 9a, the other in Ḥag. 15a and b.

Taanith 9a: "R. Joḥanan once met the young son of Resh Lakish and said to him: 'Tell me thy verse'. The boy replied: 'The foolishness of man perverteth his way, and his heart fretteth against the Lord.'[32] After pondering for a while over the matter R. Joḥanan said: 'Is it possible that there is something in the Hagiographa to which Moses did not allude in the Pentateuch?' Said the boy: 'Is not this verse alluded to in the Pentateuch? Is it not written 'And their heart failed them, they turned trembling one to another, saying, What is this that God has done to us?' "[33]

---

29 Cf. J. Meg. 3, 1; J. Keth. 13, 1; cf. also Song R. 5, 12.

30 E.g., Lev. R. 2, 1; Shab. 119b; Pes. 49b; Sanh. 17b; B. Bathra 8b, 21a, a.e.

31 Cf. Meg. 28b; Ḥag. 15a-15b; Taan. 9a; Giṭ. 56a, 68a and Ḥul. 95b.

32 Prov. 19, 3.

33 Gen. 42, 28. The boy meant that this verse expresses the same truth as Prov. 19, 3. For Joseph's brethren committed a folly in selling their brother and yet they complained about what "God had done" unto them. Cf. A. Clarke and F. Delitzsch on Prov. 19, 3.

Ḥag. 15a: "Our Rabbis taught: Once Aḥer was riding . . . and R. Meir was walking behind him . . . (R. Meir) prevailed upon him and took him to a schoolhouse. (Aḥer) said to a child: 'Recite for me thy verse'[34]. (The child) answered: 'There is no peace, saith the Lord, unto the wicked'.[35] He then took him to another schoolhouse. (Aḥer) said to a child: 'Recite for me thy verse'. He answered: 'For though thou wash thee with nitre and take thee much soap, yet thine iniquity is marked before me, saith the Lord God'.[36] He took him to yet another schoolhouse and (Aḥer) said to a child: 'Recite for me thy verse'. And he answered: 'And thou, that art spoiled, what doest thou, that thou clothest thyself with scarlet, that thou deckest thee with ornaments of gold, that thou enlargest thine eyes with paint? In vain doest thou make thyself fair,[37] etc.' He took him to yet another schoolhouse, making in all thirteen schools; all of them quoted in similar vein. When he said to the last one: 'Recite for me thy verse', he answered: 'But unto the wicked God saith, What has thou to do to declare My statutes,[38] etc.' "

These two passages, as well as such an expression in the Talmud as: זיל קרי בי רב הוא "Go and learn it (in the Bible) at school",[39] suggest the familiarity of many children

---

34 I.e., the verse which thou hast studied to-day. The answer thus obtained was considered to have the authority of an oracle, cf. Giṭ. 56a and 68a, and particularly Ḥul. 95b.

35 Is. 48, 22.

36 Jer. 2, 22.

37 Jer. 4, 30.

38 Ps. 50, 16.

39 Sanh. 33b; Sheb. 5a and 14b.

with Scripture. Reference may also be made to a passage, in Sheb. 5a, where in the course of a Halakic discussion the following pertinent question and answer occur: "Is there anyone who has not even the knowledge[40] gained at school? Yes, it is possible in the case of a child who was taken into captivity among heathen", i.e., who was thus deprived of elementary instruction in the Bible. In no other circumstance was it conceivable that one could grow up without knowledge of the Biblical verse. From the passages in Ḥag. 15a and in Taan. 9a it is safe to infer that numerous primary schools were established, in which Bible study was not limited to the Pentateuch, but included also the Prophets and the Hagiographa.[41] There is express evidence of this in J. Meg. 3, 1, where we are told: "There existed in Jerusalem four hundred and eighty synagogues, each of which was provided with a Beth-Sefer and a Beth-Talmud," i.e., a school for Biblical instruction and a school for the instruction in the Oral Law (בית ספר למקרא ובית תלמוד למדרש).[42]

A 2nd-century Rabbi testifies: "There were four hundred synagogues in the town of Bethar, in each of which were four hundred elementary teachers, and each had four hundred pupils; and when the enemy prevailed, the children, wrapped in their books, were burned in fire".[43] Since the Mishnah and Talmud had not yet been reduced to writing, the word "books" can only mean the

40 Of a Biblical law.

41 As seen from the texts quoted by the children.

42 See also Lam. R. 2, 4; Song R. 5, 12; J. Keth. 13, 1.

43 Giṭ. 58a; Lam. R. 2, 4.

Books of the Bible.[44] Allowing for some exaggeration in these narratives, there can be no doubt that the teaching of Bible to children was intensive.[45]

Because of the fluent knowledge of the Bible acquired by the Rabbis in their early training they were enabled to proceed further and develop their Halakic and Haggadic exegesis. Their familiarity with Scripture is demonstrated not only by its direct use for exegetical purposes, but also, indirectly, by many anecdotes scattered throughout Rabbinic literature. What is more, in recorded conversations and correspondence the language and idiom of the Hebrew Bible are faithfully reproduced.

An interesting anecdote is related in Ḳoheleth R. 7, 8 (also in Jerushalmi, quoted in Tosafoth Ḥag. 15a): "At the circumcision of Aḥer, when the people got merry, R. Eliezer and R. Joshua said to one another, 'Let the people carry on their business and let us go to ours'; and they began with discussions on the Pentateuch; from the Pentateuch they switched to the Prophets and from the Prophets to the Hagiographa".[46]

As examples of the apt use of Scriptural language in ordinary conversation the following are of interest:

---

44 Cf. also Keth. 105a, where a 3rd-century Rabbi refers to the existence in Jerusalem of three hundred and ninety-four elementary schools and the same number of academies for advanced study.

45 Cf. I. B. Levinsohn, 'Te'uddah Beyisroel', Warsaw, 1878, chaps. 4-6.

46 In Song R. to 1, 10 several Rabbis are recorded as being engaged in "drawing parallels between Biblical passages to explain one by another, comparing verses of the Pentateuch with verses of the Prophets and Prophets with Hagiographa".

Erub. 63a: "R. Eliezer predicted, concerning one of his pupils who decided a Halakah in his presence, that he would die in a short time.[47] When his wife asked him if he were a prophet he replied, in the words of Amos 7, 14: לא נביא ולא בן נביא אנכי 'I am no prophet, neither am I a prophet's son' ".

Taanith 4b: "Ulla, in expressing disagreement with the opinion of R. Ḥisda on a Halakah, describes it, in the words of Prov. 10, 26, "As vinegar to the teeth, and as smoke to the eyes".[48]

Some idea of the extraordinary familiarity of some of the Rabbis with Scripture may be seen from a passage in J. Meg. 3, 2, where it is recorded that in their correspondence they deliberately inverted the order of the Biblical texts so as to comply with the law that "no more than three words (from the Bible) may be written without traced lines".[49]

All this establishes that the Rabbinic scholars received a thorough training in the plain meaning of Scripture, but it does not follow that all possessed the same degree of

---

47 "Whoever decides a Halakah in the presence of his teacher incurs the penalty of death", Ber. 31b.

48 Other examples are the following: Prov. 21, 30 in Ber. 19b; Is. 7, 25 in Peah 2, 2; Ps. 107, 26 in B. Bathra 73b; Is. 30, 21 in Shab. 153a; Neh. 8, 10 in Beẓ. 15b; Prov. 4, 24 in Yeb. 24b; Prov. 24, 17 in Aboth 4, 24; Ps. 119, 97 in Men. 18a. Examples of the use of Scripture in correspondence: Joel, 4, 3 in Giṭ. 6b; Ps. 39, 2; 37, 7 in Giṭ. 7a; Hos. 9, 1 in Giṭ. 7a; Obad. 1, 15 (with a slight change) in Giṭ. 40a; Ex. 14, 11 in J. Pes. 3, 7; Job 8, 7 in J. Meg. 3, 2.

49 Giṭ. 6b.

Biblical scholarship.[50] The renowned R. Judah (Editor of the Mishnah) confesses to a lapse of memory: "I had the Scriptural text,[51] but I have forgotten it".[52] Such lapses of memory—if they can be so called—which are quite understandable, do not affect our conclusions.[53]

While the standard of Biblical knowledge amongst the Rabbis in general was high, there were some who were recognised in the Talmud as exceptionally expert, e.g., R. Ḥanina,[54] R. Eliezer b. R. Simeon,[55] Rab, Samuel and R. Joshua.[56] These were known as קראי. We are told[57] that the distinction of קרא was not attained by a scholar, עד דקרי באורייתא נביאי וכתובי בדיוקא "until he was able to read the Pentateuch, Prophets and Hagiographa with exactitude".[58]

The proficiency of the Rabbis and their meticulous study of the Bible, as well as their desire to preserve the

---

50 Cf. Tosafoth B. Bathra 113a s.v. תרווייהו.

51 I.e., upon which to base a particular decision.

52 Cf. Ab. Zarah 52b; Zeb. 59a.

53 Z. H. Chajes ('Introduction to the Talmud' ch. 17) suggested from a passage in B. Ḳamma 55a that R. Ḥija did not know the full text of Deut. 5, 16. But it is highly improbable that the Rabbi, who was also a Bible teacher, (Cf. Keth. 8b and 103b) was ignorant of such a well-known verse, occurring as it does in the Decalogue. It is probably just another such lapse or slip, or that the Rabbi was not interested in the particular Haggadic question put to him and desired to divert the conversation, an explanation to which the phraseology of the context lends force.

54 Taan. 27b.

55 Lev. R. 30, 1.

56 Ab. Zarah 40a; Yalḳuṭ Hos. §533.

57 Ḳid. 49a.

58 Of course, with full understanding.

text unimpaired, are exemplified in the attention devoted by them to Massorah. In Nedarim 37b we find the statement מקרא סופריב, עטור סופרים, כתיב ולא קרי, קרי ולא כתיב, הלכה למשה מסיני "The textual reading as transmitted by the Soferim, their stylistic embellishments, (words) read (in the text) but not written, and words written but omitted in the reading, are all Halakah from Moses at Sinai".

The arrangement of the holy writings and their authorship are dealt with by the Rabbis in detail. The passage in the Babylonian Talmud,[59] explaining the order of the twenty-four books, is regarded by modern scholars as the *locus classicus*. "The Rabbis supply here a highly characteristic explanation"[60] concerning the sequence of the books of the Hebrew Bible.

Scripture is divided by the Rabbis into three main parts תורה (Law), נביאים (Prophets) and כתובים (Hagiographa).[61] The number of books constituting the Hebrew Bible is, according to the Rabbis, twenty-four.[62] The Five Books of Moses were called חמשה חומשי תורה or merely Ḥumshin.[63] The third part, the Hagiographa, the Rabbis subdivided into smaller and larger (כתובים גדולים and קטנים).[64]

---

59 B. Bathra 14b.

60 H. E. Ryle, 'The Canon of the Old Testament', London, 1904, 2nd ed., p. 237.

61 Ḳid. 49a, a.e.

62 Taanith 8a; Ex. R. 41, 5; Num. R. 14, 18; cf. also Ḳoh. R. on 12, 11-12.

63 Ḥag. 14a; J. Meg. 1, 8; Men. 30a.

64 Ber. 57b; cf. also Soṭa 7b; Ab. dr. Nathan, ch. 40.

The division of the Pentateuch into open and closed sections, is already mentioned in the Mishnah.[65]

The old maxim: "Any verse which Moses had not divided, we may not divide"[66] shows that the Rabbis adhered to an established system of verse division. In addition, they were particularly interested in teaching the children the values of punctuation signs or accents, the arrangement of words into clauses in accordance with the sense.[67] Such instruction known as פיסוק טעמים[68] was a special part of the Rabbinical curriculum.[69] The teacher was supposed to point all this out to his scholars.[70] Reference is made by the Rabbis to passages in which the subordination of one clause to another is undecided.[71] They also refer to מקראות שאין להם הכרע, "Passages in which the grammatical construction is undecided", i.e., where from the syntactical construction of certain passages it cannot be decided whether a word is to be connected either with the preceding or with the following words.[72]

---

65 Cf. Taanith 4, 3; Ber. 2, 2; Meg. 3, 4; Tamid 5, 1; Yadaim 3, 5 and in many other places in the Talmud.

66 Meg. 22a; cf. the Mishnah Meg. 4, 4.

67 In this connection cf. Appendix, comment on Gen. 31, 52.

68 "The division of words into clauses in accordance with the sense, punctuation", Jastrow s.v. פיסוק.

69 Cf. Ned. 37a.

70 Ber. 62a. Cf. Rashi ad loc. s.v. טעמי תורה cf. Ḥag. 6b.

71 See, e.g., Ber. 60a ref. to Ps. 112, 7; 63a ref. to Ps. 119, 126; cf. Sanh. 70a referring to Prov. 23, 29-30 where the subordination of one verse to another is undecided.

72 Yoma 52a; J. Ab. Zarah 2, 7; Gen. R. 80, 6; Song R. 1, 2. See Introduction to 'Sefer Hamilim', (Hebrew Concordance Wilna 1908); I. H. Weiss, Commentary, on Mek. B'shall. Cf. Sept. on Gen. 34, 7.

Notice was taken of uncertainties in some passages, e.g., "The near Kinsman said unto Boaz, Buy it for thyself.[73] And he drew off his shoe",[74] (וישלוף נעלו)—it is not known, from the text, the Rabbis observed,[75] who actually drew off his shoe. Similarly, in the text[76] ". . . when Jeroboam went out of Jerusalem, that the prophet Ahijah . . . found him in the way; והוא מתכסה בשלמה חדשה",[77] it is not decided from the text who clad himself with a new garment, Ahijah or Jeroboam.[78]

---

73 A. V. renders 'So he drew off his shoe'.

74 Ruth 4, 8.

75 Ruth R. 7, 12; cf. B. Meẓ. 47a. Ibn Ezra, on Gen. 44, 22 in referring to this text as one of the מקראות שאין להם הכרע probably overlooked this Rabbinic passage; he also, seemingly, failed to distinguish between texts as such and the kind of uncertainties under consideration.

76 1 Kings 11, 29.

77 The Sept., Vulg. and Pesh. have ואחיה instead of והוא so R. V., Ewald understands Jeroboam to be meant.

78 Ruth R. 7, 12, so Ḳimḥi ad loc. Cf. C. F. Burney ad loc. For further illustrations of this kind of uncertainties cf. Midrash ibid and Ḥul. 92a ref. to Hos. 12, 5. In this connection cf. Appendix, comments on Gen. 4, 4; 10, 12; 18, 3; 28, 13; 47, 31a; Ex. 22, 12; 22, 27; Num. 5, 18a; 19, 2; 1 Kings 11, 29.

CHAPTER FIVE

THE RABBIS' APPRECIATION OF PESHAṬ

PART ONE

PART TWO

PART ONE

A. GRAMMAR

B. ETYMOLOGY

C. LEXICOLOGY

D. SYNONYMS

A. GRAMMAR

Consonants

Vocalisation

The Article

Prepositional prefixes

Pronominal suffixes

Absolute and construct state

The Numerals

Further parts of Speech:

1. Particles
2. Separate Prepositions
3. The ו׳

Old accusative ending, also called He locale

THE VERB

Derived forms:

1. Qal
2. Niph'al
3. Pi'el
4. Pu'al
5. Hiph'il
6. Hoph'al
7. Hithpa'el

Quadriliterals

Biliteral basic stems

Infinitive absolute

Tenses

Participle

Gender

Person

Number

Disagreement between the members of a sentence

Grammatical terminology

CHAPTER FIVE

THE RABBIS' APPRECIATION OF PESHAṬ

In this chapter some interesting illustrations of the Rabbis' appreciation of Peshaṭ, drawn directly from the Rabbinic sources will be presented. For reasons already explained, these illustrations emerge only after a careful sifting of the vast store of Rabbinic learning.[1] While the results cover a considerable variety of subject-matter, they do not claim to represent anything more than one further contribution to a subject which, unfortunately, has not yet received the attention it merits.[2] It is hoped that the material here collected will serve to show the importance of the contribution of the Rabbis to the objective study of the Bible.

This material, for convenience, is divided into two parts. Neither is self-contained, nor intended to be exhaustive in scope. In the first part, dealing with more particularised aspects of exegesis, consideration is given to points of grammar, etymology, lexicology and synonyms; the second part is concerned with critical Rabbinical analyses of the text and other matters of broader import. Besides these special features of Peshaṭ considered in this chapter,

---

1 Cf. supra p. 80.
2 Cf. Foreword to this work by R. T. Herford.

there are numerous comments and interpretations scattered throughout the Rabbinic literature which exhibit a marked appreciation of Peshaṭ; examples of such exegesis are set out in an Appendix.[3]

It is important, too, to observe that, though Rabbinic handling of a text may bear, on occasions, the character of Midrashic[4] interpretation, there is an underlying core of objective fact. This phenomenon is perhaps best illustrated in the grammatical notes found in the Talmud and Midrash; the grammatical point is noted, even though it is used for the purpose of conveying some other Midrashic or moral idea. We must never lose sight of the fact that the Rabbis did not, and indeed could not, possess the critical apparatus and experience now available to modern scholars. Their observations must therefore be regarded in the light of an early contribution to the study of the Bible and, as such merit prominence in the history of Biblical exegesis.

3 The examples, which are set out in chronological order, relate mainly to Pentateuchal texts.

4 Cf. supra p. 48.

A. GRAMMAR

Selected items of Hebrew grammar, to which attention is called in Rabbinic literature may conveniently be classified under the following heads: (a) Consonants, (b) Vocalisation, (c) The Article, (d) Prepositional prefixes, (e) Pronominal suffixes, (f) Absolute and construct state, (g) the Numerals, (h) further Parts of speech: 1. Particles, 2. Separate Prepositions, 3. The ו׳, (i) Old accusative ending, also called He locale. To the Verb, because of its importance, we devote a separate section, following an examination of the above-mentioned points of grammar.

(a) *Consonants:* Reference is made by the Rabbis to the names of the Hebrew letters, their alphabetical order[1] and their numerical[2] value. There are some notes on the formation[3] of some of the Hebrew characters. For example, "the beth is closed at the sides but open in front"; also "a beth ב has two projecting points, one pointing upward and one below at the back"[4] (this would refer to the backward projection of the ב, whereby it differs from

1 Shab. 104a. Cf. Shab. 103b; Gen. R. 1, 11.

2 Cf. Gen. R. 43, 2 and 91, 2; Num. R. 13, 16 and 18, 21; Shab. 70a; Yoma 20a and76a; Nazir 5a; Ḥul. 139b, a.e.

3 Gen. R. 1, 10; 12, 10; J. Ber. 1, 9; Shab. 103b and 104a.

4 Gen. R. 1, 10.

the Kaf, thus: ב and כ). "The He ה is closed in all sides and open underneath . . ." and "at the side".[5] "The Yod י has a bent (curved) back".[5] "The foot of the Ḳuf ק is suspended".[6] The medial Mem is referred to as "open" and the final as "closed". The medial forms of כ' נ' פ' צ' are referred to as "bent" and their finals as "straight" letters.[7] A warning is given against confusing certain letters, e.g., א with ע,[8] ב with כ, ג with צ, ד with ר, ה with ח, ו with י, ז with final ן, final ם with ס.[9] The Rabbis say: "It is written, 'Hear O Israel the Lord our God the Lord is One'—(אחד) if you make (the letter) ד 'daleth' into (the letter) ר 'resh'[10] you cause the destruction of the whole Universe. It is written, כי לא תשתחוה לאל אחר 'For thou shalt bow down to no other god'.[11] If you change the 'resh' into a 'daleth',[12] you bring, as a result, destruction upon the world. It is written, 'And ye shall not profane (תחללו) My holy name'[13]; if you make the letter 'heth' into the letter 'he',[14] you bring as a result destruction upon the world".[15]

5 Gen. R. 12, 10.
6 Shab. 104a.
7 Cf. Shab. 103b, 104a.
8 I.e., which have a like pronunciation (Rashi, Shab. 103b).
9 Cf. Lev. R. 19, 2; Shab. 103b; Erub. 13a.
10 Reading אחר (strange) instead of אחד (one).
11 Ex. 34, 14.
12 The text would then read: thou shalt not bow down to the one God.
13 Lev. 22, 32.
14 Reading לא תהללו ye shall not praise, instead of לא תחללו ye shall not profane.
15 Lev. R. 19, 2; for further illustrations cf. Lev. R. ad loc.

The final forms of כ׳ מ׳ נ׳ פ׳ צ׳ are combined in the mnemonic מנצפ״ך.[16]

The greatest care is demanded of the professional scribe. R. Ishmael spoke thus to R. Meir (a professional scribe): "My son, be careful in thy work, as it is a heavenly work, lest thou err in omitting or adding one iota, and so cause the destruction of the whole world".[17]

R. Ḥisda, discovering R. Ḥananeel writing a Sefer-Torah from memory, said to him: "Indeed thou art able to write the whole Torah by heart, but our Sages have forbidden the writing of even one letter without an exemplar".[18]

Anomalies in the Massoretic text are noted, e.g., final Mem in middle of the word;[19] suspended letters;[20] majuscular[21] and minuscular [22] letters; a letter curtailed;[23] letters missing;[24] or superfluous;[25] inverted Nun.[26] Refer-

16 Cf. Gen. R. 1, 11; Shab. 103b and 104a and Meg. 2b.

17 Erub. 13a, and see the ensuing discussion and Rashi l.c.

18 Meg. 18b. We are told in Keth. 106a that there were paid correctors of Biblical books among the officers of the Temple.

19 Sanh. 94a, ref. to Is. 9, 6.

20 Lev. R. 13, 5 ref. to Ps. 80, 13; Sanh. 103b, ref. to Job 38, 15; cf. B. Bath. 109b ref. to Jud. 18, 30.

21 Cf. Soferim ch. 9; cf. Ḳid. 30a ref. to Lev. 11, 43.

22 Lev. R. 23, 12 ref. to Deut. 32, 18.

23 Ḳid. 66b ref. to Num. 25, 12.

24 Hor. 13a ref. to Num. 15, 24.

25 Cf. Gen. R. 41, 6 ref. to Gen. 13, 9; Gen. R. 3, 8 ref. to Is. 44, 24; Num. R. 15, 4 ref. to Ex. 25, 31; cf. Ibn Ezra on Is. 44, 24 (Friedlander's ed.) London, 1873, and Ḳimḥi ad loc. Cf. also M. Mendelssohn on Gen. 13, 9.

26 Shab. 115b.

ence is made also to dots or points found over single letters in the Bible.[27]

(b) *Vocalisation:* The importance given to correct vocalisation[28] is seen in many references to קרי[29] and כתיב[30] as well as to אם למקרא ואם למסורת.[31] In discussions about Miḳra and Massora the Rabbis had recourse to the principle, referred to in the Talmud,[32] that the correct meaning of a word is to be decided by the context as a whole. Thus e.g., בחלב[33] in לא תבשל גדי בחלב אמו—which might read בְּחֵלֶב ("fat") or בַּחֲלֵב from חָלָב ("milk")—the preceding word תבשל ("seething") determines the reading in favour of the latter;[34] וטמאה שבעים[35] which might read שְׁבֻעַיִם ("two weeks") or שִׁבְעִים ("seventy")—the following word כנדתה shows that the proper reading is שְׁבֻעַיִם.[36]

---

27 As to the origin and significance of these points it is stated: "When Elias will come and ask Ezra, why has thou written thus? He will answer, I have long ago pointed these letters; but when Elias will say unto him, thou hast written well, then he will remove these dots", (Num. R. 3, 13).

28 In this connection cf. Appendix, comments on Gen. 47, 31b; Deut. 25, 19.

29 The Massoretic instruction for reading.

30 The traditional spelling of Biblical words. Cf. e.g., Gen. R. 34, 8; Ex. R. 30, 24; Lev. R. 19, 6; Sanh. 20a; Soṭa 31a a.e.

31 Cf. e.g., Pes. 86b; Suk. 6b; Ḳid. 18b; Sanh. 4a and b; Mak. 7a; Zeb. 38a; Bek. 34a; Kerith. 17b. Cf. supra p. 97, references to signs of punctuation or accents.

32 Cf. Yeb. 102b ref. to Deut. 25, 9; Mak. 8a ref. to Lev. 25, 26 and to Deut. 19, 5; B. Meẓia 56b ref. to Num. 21, 26. Cf. infra p. 144 and note 43.

33 Ex. 23, 19.

34 Sanh. 4b.

35 Lev. 12, 5.

36 Zeb. 38a.

(c) *The Article:* The article indicates a person or thing specific, distinctive or unique, e.g., הירך[37]—"the" hip—means the special hip, i.e., the right hip which is the stronger of the two;[38] הזרוע[39] "the" arm means the right arm;[40] יום הששי[41] "the" sixth day means the sixth day of Sivan;[42] השמים והארץ[43]—with the addition of the article in the words viz., *"the* heaven" and *"the* earth" the text indicates that reference is made to the previously — planned heaven and earth.[44] Where a substantive is defined by the article, its attribute also takes the article; thus in referring to הכבש אחד[45] the Rabbis ask: "If it says הכבש why does it say אחד"[46] (and not האחד).[47]

(d) *Prepositional Prefixes:* Prepositional prefixes are noted, for example, in the following instruction given in connection with the divine Names that are not to be erased: "Our Sages taught: That which is joined to the

---

37 Gen. 32, 33.
38 Ḥul. 91a.
39 Deut. 18, 3.
40 Ḥul. 134b.
41 Gen. 1, 31.
42 Shab. 88a; Ab. Zarah 3a. Cf. supra, p. 106.
43 Gen. 1, 1; Is. 66, 22.
44 Gen. R. 1, 13.
45 Num. 28, 4.
46 Meg. 28a. Cf. Ibn Ezra; J. H. Mecklenburg, 'Ha-Ketab weha-Ḳabbalah' on Num. 28, 4; S. R. Driver on 1 Sam. 8, 17; and Ibn Ezra on Ex. 29, 39. The grammatical term ה' הידיעה is mentioned in Zohar quoted by M. Mendelssohn on Gen. 1, 31. In all the cases quoted above it is quite clear that the Rabbinic constructions were based on the use of the definite article.
47 Cf. B. Epstein, 'Torah T'mima', on Num. 28, 4.

Name, whether before it or after it,[48] may be erased. Before it: how? *To* the Lord: the *lamed* ל ('to') . . .; *in* the Lord: the *beth* ב ('in') . . .; *and* the Lord: the waw ו ('and') . . .; *from* the Lord: the *mem* מ ('from') . . .; *that* the Lord: the *shin* ש ('that') . . .; interrogative *he* before the Lord: the *he* ה . . .; *as* the Lord: the *Kaph* כ ('as') may be erased".[49]

Detailed meanings of prepositional prefixes are noted as follows: E.g., "ב" may mean "at" in the sense of a definite time, בחצות—a definite time—is contrasted with כחצות which suggests an approximate time.[50]

"כ" may be used to express comparison as distinct from identity, e.g., the Rabbinic comment on כאלמנה[51] "as a widow though yet not a widow in fact".[52]

"מ" may be used in a partitive sense, e.g., the "מ" in מעיני[53] and מדבר[54] which according to the Rabbis[55] means "some of the eyes" and "part of a thing". "ל" and "מ";

---

48 Prefix or suffix.

49 Sheb. 35b.

50 Ber. 3b ref. to Ex. 11, 4; cf. Ber. 7b ref. to Ps. 37, 1. Cf. Yeb. 102b ref. to Deut. 25, 9. Reference is also made to the use of ב in the sense of conjunction, i.e., "in conjunction with", cf. B. Ḳamma 58b ref. to Ex. 22, 4. Cf. Appendix, comment on Ex. 11, 4.

51 Lam. 1, 1.

52 Sanh. 104a. Cf. Lam. R. 1, 3 where this point is illustrated by a number of examples.

53 Num. 15, 24.

54 Lev. 4, 13.

55 Hor. 4a and 5a. Cf. B. Ḳamma 54b ref. to the "ב" in בכל Deut. 14, 26 and Ned. 31a ref. to "ב" in ביצחק Gen. 21, 12 as partitive. Cf. Appendix, comment on Lev. 18, 24.

the distinction between the two is exemplified by contrasting[56] מהם (from them) with להם (to them).

(e) *Pronominal Suffixes:* The use of pronominal suffixes is noted: *(1) with the noun,* as expressing possesive pronoun; e.g., זקניו[57] as contrasted with זקנים — means זקנים משלו[58] elders of his own; חפציך[59] as contrasted with חפצים[60]—means 'thy' jewels.[61] *(2) with the verb,* as an accusative, e.g., the ה in וכבשה[62] represents the accusative third feminine suffix.[63]

The significance of the additional Nun[64] (i.e., Nun Energicum) is noted; thus יכבדנני[65] contrasted with the ordinary form signifies "כבוד אחר כבוד".[66] Further reference to pronominal suffixes is noted in the Talmudic passage alluded to earlier,[67] as follows: "After it: How?[68]

---

56 Yeb. 102b ref. to Hos. 5, 6.

57 In וכל זקניו כבוד Is. 24, 23.

58 Lev. R. 11, 8.

59 In וכל חפציך לא ישוו בה Prov. 3, 15.

60 In וכל חפצים לא ישוו בה Prov. 8, 11.

61 Gen. R. 35, 3; cf. M. Ḳaṭan 9b. F. Delitzsch ad loc. accepts the Midrashic rendering of חפציך in this text as meaning 'thy jewels'.

62 Gen. 1, 28.

63 Gen. R. 8, 12.

64 Cf. Gesenius K. § 58^4.

65 Ps. 50, 23.

66 Lev. R. 9, 2. Cf. F. Delitzsch ad loc. Cf. Sanh. 43b, 'The Soncino Press', London, 1935, note 1.

67 Under (d).

68 With reference to the statement at the beginning of the passage that the letters joined to the divine Name before or after it may be erased.

Our God: the suffix *nu* נו ('our') . . .; *their* God: the suffix *hem* הם ('their') . . .; *your* God: the suffix *Kem* כם ('your') may be erased".[69]

(f) *Absolute and Construct state:* That the substantive form may vary according to whether it is in the absolute or construct state, is clearly appreciated, e.g., ובער בשדה אחר[70] is to be read בִּשְׂדֵה אחר in the construct (in the field of another man)[71] and not בְּשָׂדֶה אחר in the absolute (in another field). A noun of the form עֶבֶד[72] however, is the same in either state; thus it is pointed out[73] that עֶבֶד עברי [74] may mean either "a servant who is a Hebrew" or "a servant of a Hebrew", i.e., a Canaanitish servant.[75] The termination ת may represent both the absolute plural and the construct singular of the feminine noun.[76]

(g) *The Numerals:* A distinction is drawn between cardinal and ordinal numbers, e.g., יום אחד[77] (one day) contrasted with יום ראשון[78] (the first day).

---

69 Sheb. 35b.

70 Ex. 22, 4.

71 B. Ḳamma 23a. The construct is implied in the context of this reference. Cf. W. Heidenheim, 'Habanath ha-Miḳrah', on Rashi Ex. 22, 4.

72 I.e., a Segolate noun.

73 Mek. on Ex. 21, 2.

74 Ex. 21, 2.

75 In this connection cf. Appendix, comment on Ex. 1, 15.

76 Cf. Hor. 4a ref. to the word מצות in Lev. 4, 13 and Suk. 32a ref. to כפת in Lev. 23, 40.

77 Gen. 1, 5.

78 Gen. R. 3, 9. In this connection cf. Appendix, comment on Gen. 14, 4.

(h) *Further parts of speech:* There are some observations on some of the uses of certain (1) particles, e.g., כי, this conjunction, according to the Rabbis, "serves for four meanings: אי (if), דלמא (perhaps), אלא (but), דהא (because)".[79] אך and רק intimate limiting qualifications. את and גם imply an extended qualification.[80] (2) Separate prepositions, e.g., את primarily used as the sign of the object,[81] also serves as a preposition meaning "along with"[82] thus contrasting תבוא את[83] with תביא את;[84] אחר and אחרי—both forms are noted and there is some speculation as to the distinction in meaning;[85] according to one authority "אחר" signifies "in connection with" and "אחרי" signifies "without connection"; על primarily used in the sense 'upon' signifies also 'near', 'by'.[86] (3) The use of "Waw" in a conjunctive sense as meaning 'and' is

---

79 R. Hash. 3a. Cf. Sheb. 49b ref. to Lev. 5, 4; Giṭ. 90a and Rashi ibid. Cf. Ex. R. 9, 1 ref. to Ex. 7, 9 where כי is contrasted with אם.

80 J. Ber. 9, 5; Gen. R. 1, 14; 53, 15; Ḥag. 12a; cf. Sanh. 59b. Cf. Gesenius K. §153. In this connection cf. Appendix, comment on Gen. 1, 1.

81 Cf. Gen. R. 1, 14; Sanh. 8a ref. to Deut. 31, 23.

82 Cf. Gesenius K. §117k. In this connection cf. Appendix, comment on Gen. 4, 1.

83 Deut. 31, 7.

84 Deut. 31, 23. Sanh. 8a. Cf. Sifre on Num. 35, 34 and Meg. 29a ref. to Deut. 30, 3.

85 Gen. R. 44, 5.

86 Men. 96a. Cf. Gen. R. 4, 3 ref. to Gen. 1, 7 and Yeb. 103a ref. to Deut. 25, 9 distinction between על and מעל. Cf. Appendix, comment on Num. 2, 20. Cf. S. Rosenblatt, 'Bible Interpretation in the Mishnah' pp. 8 and 27.

expressed in the statement,[87] "... where, however, ואלה 'and these' is used it adds something ...", i.e., forms a continuation. They also noticed the use of "Waw" in a disjunctive sense, as meaning 'or' and, as an example, reference is made to Ex. 21, 17 ומכה אביו ואמו where ואמו is interpreted as meaning 'or his mother'.[88]

(i) *Old accusative ending, also called He locale*: "ה" when placed at the end of a word denotes "motion towards", thus it is stated:[89] "To every word requiring a ל prefixed you may attach a ה as a suffix", and as instances of this we are referred to מצרימה[90] and מחנימה.[91]

---

87 Gen. R. 12, 3 a.e.

88 Sanh. 66a, 85b; B. Meẓ. 94b; Ḥul. 78b; cf. Men. 90b.

89 Yeb. 13b; Gen. R. 50, 3 a.e.

90 Gen. 12, 10.

91 2 Sam. 17, 24. A plausible interpretation of the exceptional form לשאולה (combination of prefix ל and suffix ה) in Ps. 9, 18 is given in Midrash Gen. R. 50, 3. Cf. F. Delitzsch and A. C. Jennings on Ps. ad loc. For the use of He locale extended to time, cf. Appendix, comment on Ex. 13, 10.

THE VERB

THE VERB

For convenience we may classify Rabbinic notes on the Verb under the following heads: (a) Derived forms, (b) Quadriliterals, (c) Biliteral basic stems, (d) Infinitive absolute, (e) Tenses, (f) Participle, (g) Gender, (h) Person, (i) Number.

(a) *Derived forms:* Although the Rabbis do not refer by name to the various derived forms of the verbs as conventionally used by grammarians, there can be no doubt that they were aware of the significance of each of the conjugations.

Qal is used in an active sense, e.g., תַעֲשֶׂה[92] implying תעשה ולא מן העשוי, i.e., the active form, "you must make it, but not when it is already made"[93] thus distinguishing the active form from the passive. It also represents spontaneous action as distinct from involuntary action. Thus והבאים[94] is contrasted with מוּבאים.[95]

Niph'al. The two uses of Niph'al are noted, (1) Reflexive, e.g., יִשָּׁמֵעַ would mean "obeying himself" as con-

92 Deut. 22, 12.
93 Men. 40b.
94 Gen. 7, 16.
95 Gen. R. 32, 8; Zeb. 116a. Cf. Num. R. 7, 9 ref. to Num. 5, 4.

trasted with יִשְׁמַע "hearken";[96] הִכּוֹן[97] is interpreted to mean "put thyself in proper condition";[98] (2) Passive, e.g., יֵרָאֶה[99] means "be seen" contrasted with יִרְאֶה "he shall see".[100] Both uses are indicated in the word ונמכר, viz., "he shall be sold"[101] (i.e., through the court), and "he sells himself".[102]

Pi'el as contrasted with Qal has an intensified meaning, thus עִזְּבוּ as contrasted with עָזְבוּ means "utterly abandon".[103] The Pi'el form may also have a causative significance, e.g., שָׁמֵעַ[104] "hearken", whilst the form שַׁמֵּעַ means "to cause to hear".[105]

נָשַׁל "it slipped" as contrasted with the form נִשֵּׁל meaning "it hurled away"[106] shows that a verb, though intransitive in the Qal, may be transitive in the Pi'el.

---

96 Sanh. 89a ref. to Deut. 18, 19. Cf. Gesenius §51^{2}.

97 Am. 4, 12. Cf. Fuerst s.v. כון.

98 J. Meg. 1, 9. Vide Jastrow s.v. כון. Cf. Appendix, comment on Gen. 12, 3.

99 Ex. 23, 17.

100 Ḥag. 4a; Sanh. 4b.

101 Mek. on Ex. 21, 2. ref. to ונמכר in Ex. 22, 2.

102 Mek. ibid ref. to Lev. 25, 39. Cf. Ben-Ze'eb, "Talmud Leshon Ibri", Wilna, 1879, §235.

103 Yalḳ. Hos. §527 ref. to Is. 1, 4; cf. Jastrow s.v. עזב. Cf. Mak. 11a that דבר in the Pi'el form denotes "speaking harshly".

104 Deut. 1, 16.

105 Sanh. 7b; cf. Ber. 15a ref. to שמע in Deut. 6, 4 and cf. annotations by S. Strashun ad loc.

106 Mak. 7b and Sanh. 5b ref. to Deut. 19, 5. Cf. Rashi in Mak. ibid; Jastrow s.v. ישל and M. Mielziner, "Introduction to the Talmud", 3rd ed. N.Y., 1925, p. 186.

The *Pu'al* like Niph'al has a passive significance, e.g., עֻבַּד contrasted with עָבַד.[107]

The causative significance of *Hiph'il* is well illustrated in the remark "read not וַיִּקְרָא ('and he called') but וַיַּקְרִיא ('and he made others call')".[108] As a causative the Hiph'il may govern two accusatives, e.g., ותקח[109] and ותכרת[109] if read וַתַּקַּח[110] and וַתַּכְרֵת[110] (i.e., the Hiph'il form) would imply "she caused to be taken" and "she caused it to be cut off", by asking another person to do it.[111]

The *Hiph'il* form and derived meaning were recognised by the Rabbis, e.g., יִשְׁמַע[112] (in the Qal form) if read יַשְׁמִעַ (in the Hiph'il form) would imply "to proclaim").[113]

The contrast between תביא[114] "thou shalt bring" and תבוא[115] "thou shalt come"[116] shows that a verb which is intrasitive in Qal may be transitive in Hiph'il; similarly והשיב as contrasted with ושב.[117]

---

107 Pes. 26b; B. Meẓia 30a ref. to Deut. 21, 3. Cf. B. Meẓia 30a "Soncino Press", note 8; Rashi, English trans. ed. by A. M. Silbermann, London, on Ex. 3, 2 note 3.

108 Soṭa 10a ref. to Gen. 21, 33. Cf. Sanh. 7b ref. to Ex. 23, 1.

109 Ex. 4, 25.

110 The vocalisation is from the Wilna ed. of the Talmud.

111 Ab. Zarah 27a.

112 Deut. 18, 19.

113 Sanh. 89a; cf. S. Strashun on Ber. 15a.

114 Deut. 31, 23.

115 Deut. 31, 7.

116 Sanh. 8a.

117 Sifre on Num. 35, 34; Meg. 29a ref. to Deut. 30, 3.

HOPH'AL represents the passive of Hiph'il. Thus הורד[118] (in the Hoph'al form) "he was brought down" is contrasted with הוריד (in the Hiph'il form) meaning "he did bring down".[119]

The HITHP'AEL form מתהלך[120] as contrasted with מהלך ("walking"), means "he hastened and went upward".[121]

(b) QUADRILITERALS: Some quadriliteral words are treated as compounds (i.e., formed by composition and contraction of two stems), whilst others are explained by the aid of cognate languages, e.g., ברשע[122] from בן רשע[123] ("wicked son"); רעואל[124] from רע אל[125] ("friend of God"); בליעל[126] from בלי על[127] ("without a yoke"); גלמודה[128] from the Arabic;[129] סלסליה[130] from the Aramaic;[131] אברך[132] from the Greek.[133]

---

118 Gen. 39, 1.
119 Soṭa 13b. Cf. Ex. R. 25, 5 and B. Meẓiah 86b ref. to Gen. 18, 4.
120 Gen. 3, 8.
121 Gen. R. 19, 7; Cf. Jastrow s.v. הלך.
122 Gen. 14, 2.
123 Gen. R. 42, 5. Cf. Gesenius Heb. and Chal. Lex. s.v. ברשע and S. R. Driver on the text. Cf. Appendix, comment on Gen. 14, 2.
124 Ex. 2, 18. Cf. Appendix, comment on Ex. 2, 18.
125 Ex. R. 1, 32; cf. S. R. Driver on the text.
126 Deut. 13, 14.
127 Sifre ad loc.; Sanh. 111b; cf. Gesenius K. §81d; G. A. Smith on Deut. 13, 14. Cf. Ber. 4a ref. to 2 Sam. 4, 4; Sanh. 105a ref. to בלעם. Cf. infra p. 136 note 22.
128 Is. 49, 21. Cf. infra p. 137.
129 Gen. R. 79, 7; cf. R. Hash. 26a and Soṭa 42a.
130 Prov. 4, 8. Cf. infra p. 137 and note 35.
131 R. Hash. 26b; Meg. 18a.
132 Gen. 41, 43. Cf. infra p. 137.
133 Mek. on Deut. 1, 1 (quoted in J.E. and in Heb. Encyclopedia 'Oẓar Yisrael', s.v. Abrech).

(c) BILITERAL BASIC STEMS: Triliteral stems, in some instances, would appear to be traced back by the Rabbis to a biliteral base, e.g., סכך and נסך from סך;[134] בלה, בלל, בלע and also the prepositions בלתי, בלי are formed from a biliteral stem בל;[135] re-duplications are considered as signifying emphasis, e.g., ירקרק and אדמדם[136] denote deep green and deep red respectively.[137]

(d) INFINITIVE ABSOLUTE: Note is taken of the use of the infinitive absolute to denote intensification when immediately preceding a finite verb, e.g., הוכח תוכיח,[138] השב תשיבם[139] and שלח תשלח[140] imply "even a hundred times".[141]

(e) TENSES: The tenses of the verb, if they may be so called, attracted the attention of the Rabbis; there is special reference to the past ("לשעבר")[142] and the future

---

134 Cf. Num. R. 4, 14 ref. to Ex. 25, 29; Ber. 62b ref. to 1 Sam. 24, 4; Men. 97a.

135 Cf. J. Ber. 6, 1 ref. to Ps. 16, 20; Lev. R. 19, 2 ref. to 1 Sam. 2, 2; Taan. 9a ref. to Mal. 3, 10. Cf. Fuenn, 'Ha-Ozar', note on בלת. Cf. Sanh. 108b comparing וישכן Gen. 8, 1 with שככה Est. 7, 10. Cf. Ibn Ezra on Ex. 4, 31; 34, 8; W. Heidenheim, 'Habanath ha-Miḳrah', on Rashi Ex. 25, 29 note 1.

136 Lev. 13, 39.

137 Sifra ad loc.; Mishnah Neg. 11, 4; cf. Rashi, Ibn Ezra and M. Mendelssohn on the text.

138 Lev. 19, 17.

139 Deut. 22, 1.

140 Deut. 22, 7.

141 B. Meẓia 31a.

142 Soṭa 46b; Pes. 7a and b; cf. Gen. R. 22, 5.

("להבא").[143] Thus יקריב[144] as contrasted with הקריב, refers to the future ("מכאן ולהבא").[145] It is also observed that in some cases the imperfect form is used where ordinarily one would expect the perfect, e.g., אז ישיר[146] instead of שר;[147] יבנה[148] instead of בנה.[149] Similarly, the verbs תלבשני, תקפיאני, תתיכני and תשככני[150] are in the imperfect form though they have the significance of the perfect.[151]

In one case we are told that the perfect is used in place of an imperfect, e.g., נתתי[152] instead of אתן, the explanation adduced being that "the promise of God is as an accomplished fact."[153]

Attention is drawn to the use of the "Waw consecutive" when connected with the verb, in the Rabbinic comment on ויהי (with waw) contrasting it with יהי.[154] Of special interest is the reference to the use of the imperfect

---

143 Soṭa ibid; Pes. ibid.

144 Lev. 7, 11.

145 Lev. R. 9, 6. Cf. discussion in Soṭa 46b whether יעבד and יזרע Deut. 21, 4 denote the future or the past.

146 Ex. 15, 1. Cf. Rashi ad loc.

147 Sanh. 91b.

148 Deut. 25, 9.

149 Yeb. 10b.

150 Job 10, 10-11.

151 Gen. R. 4, 5. Cf. the E.V. Cf. also Lange on Job 10, 10-11, that "the imperfects in this verse and in the following have their time determined by the perfects of verses 8, 9". Cf. also Ewald on the text.

152 Gen. 15, 18.

153 Gen. R. 44, 22. For further illustrations of this kind see ibid.

154 Ex. R. 23, 15.

to indicate a continuous present, e.g., יזיד[155] the meaning being that the offender continues with wilful intent even after being warned.[156]

(f) PARTICIPLE: Continuity is also expressed by the participle — e.g., Rabbinic comments on מקושש[157] "continuing to gather"[158] and מתנבאים[159] "continuing to prophesy".[160]

Particular notice was taken by the Rabbis of the use in the Bible of Gender, Person and Number in connection with various forms.

(g) GENDER: The distinction of the masculine and feminine gender of the Noun, Adjective, Verb and Number may be seen from the following examples: שירה (song) is "לשון נקבה" (fem.) and שיר is "זכר" (masc.);[161] אותו[162] "intimates the masculine gender" ("זכר");[163] זוֹנָה (fem.) contrasted with זוֹנֶה (masc.);[164] יכולת[165] is contrasted with יכול;[166] יורוך and יאמרו[167] contrasted with תורך and תאמר;[168] יקח contrasted with תקח.[169]

---

155 Ex. 21, 14 instead of הזיד.
156 Sanh. 41a, cf. Rashi ibid.
157 Num. 15, 33.
158 Sanh. 41a.
159 Num. 11, 27.
160 Sanh. 17a.
161 Ex. R. 23, 11.
162 Lev. 22, 28.
163 Ḥul. 78b.
164 Tem. 29b ref. to Deut. 23, 19.
165 Num. 14, 16.
166 Ber. 32a.
167 Deut. 17, 11.
168 Song R. on Song 1, 2.
169 Ḳid. 4b ref. to Deut. 24, 1.

Note was taken of epicene nouns, thus e.g., commenting on דרך "a way", which "usually is used in feminine gender"[170] ("לשון נקבה"), it is pointed out that "we find (in the Bible) דרך in the masculine gender" ("לשון זכר")[171] e.g., in the phrase בדרך אחד.[172]

The fact that the same form is used for both second person masculine and third person feminine of the singular imperfect gave rise to different constructions on the word תרונה[173].

(h) PERSON: E.g., אזכיר[174] contrasted with תזכיר;[175] יסתר[176] contrasted with נסתר;[177] commenting on ואמר[178] and ותחס[179] it is pointed out that "it should read ואמרתי and וחסתי."[179] Two different constructions are put on the word

---

170 Ḳid. 2b.

171 Ḳid. 2b. ref. to Ex. 18, 20 and Deut. 28, 25. The Rabbis explain in an attractive way why דרך is used in each case in a different gender. Cf. ibid Tosafoth s.v. קשו. Cf. Gesenius K. §122b and 1.

172 Deut. 28, 7.

173 M. Ḳaṭan 16b ref. to Prov. 1, 20. Cf. מירא דכיא (by Mordecai b. Jehiel, Jozefov, 1878) on Rashi Gen. 3, 4. Cf. F. Delitzsch on Prov. 1, 20; Gesen. K. §124e.

174 Ex. 20, 24.

175 J. Ber. 4, 4. RITBA, quoted in Midrash Shmuel on Aboth 2, 7, suggests that א interchanges with ת.

176 Gen. 31, 49.

177 Gen. R. 74, 14.

178 1 Sam. 24, 11.

179 Num. R. 4, 20; Ber. 62b. The reading of ואמר by Jerome and ואחס by the Sept., Targum and Pesh. agree with the Rabbinic observation. Cf. S. R. Driver ad loc. and Gesen. K. §144⁰.

ממנו,[180] since the same form is used for both first person plural and third person masculine singular.

(i) NUMBER: E.g., that תשחטו[181] "signifies two";[182] אותו[183] "denotes one but not two";[184] ויחן[185] contrasted with ויחנו;[186] בצלמו,[187] ברא,[188] ויאמר,[189] אליו,[190] הוא,[191] יודע[191] are contrasted with their plurals;[192] דם contrasted with דמי.[193]

Comment is made on the employment in the Bible of Nouns and Verbs to express the plural in a collective sense. Thus, referring to the substantives שור וחמור[194] (generic singular) employed in the text to signify the plural, the Rabbis pointed out that it is customary to speak of many oxen and many asses as one ox and one ass.[195] Commenting on ויאמר עד[196] where ויאמרו[197] might be

---

180 Soṭa 35a ref. to Num. 13, 31. Cf. Rashi, English translation ed. by A. M. Silbermann, London, on Num. 13, 31, note 3. Cf. Ber. 5a ref. to Ps. 94, 12.

181 Lev. 22, 28.

182 Ḥul. 82a.

183 Lev. 22, 28.

184 Ḥul. 78b.

185 Ex. 19, 2.

186 Lev. R. 9, 9.

187 Gen. 1, 27.

188 Gen. 1, 1.

189 Gen. 1, 6.

190 Deut. 4, 7.

191 Josh. 22, 22.

192 Gen. R. 8, 9; Deut. R. 2, 13; J. Ber. 9, 1; Cf. also Keth. 5a.

193 Gen. R. 22, 9; Sanh. 37a ref. to Gen. 4, 11.

194 Gen. 32, 6.

195 Gen. R. 75, 6.

196 1 Sam. 12, 5.

197 Mak. 23b. Cf. Targ. and other versions, quoted by S. R. Driver, that render it in the plural.

expected, they say "Samuel may have taken all Israel collectively, using the singular expression (verb)".[198]

NOTE: The Rabbis also concerned themselves with cases in which there is an *apparent disagreement* between the members of a sentence in respect of (a) Gender and (b) Number, thus:

(a) GENDER: commenting on חטאת רובץ[199] they expected רובצת;[200] instead of יורוך and יאמרו[201] there should have been תורך and תאמר, if they were to be construed with the preceding word תורה;[202] the verb תבעה must be construed with the following Noun אש but not with the preceding מים;[203] if דרך is feminine gender then it must be שלש דרכים and not שלשה.[204]

(b) NUMBER: in the text, קדושים הוא, המה is expected instead of הוא;[205] instead of ובני דן חושים[206] should be . . . ובן;[207] ידיו יצרו[208] cannot be read as ידו since its predicate is in the plural.[209]

---

198 Mak. ibid.

199 Gen. 4, 7.

200 Gen. R. 22, 6. Cf. G. J. Spurrell on Gen. 4, 7 quoting various critics emending the text.

201 Deut. 17, 11.

202 Song R. on Song 1, 2.

203 B. Ḳamma 4b ref. to Is. 46, 1. Cf. Keth. 65b ref. to 1 Sam. 1, 9.

204 Ḳid. 2b.

205 Gen. R. 8, 9 ref. to Josh. 24, 19.

206 Gen. 46, 23.

207 B. Bath. 143b. Cf. Ibn Ezra and M. Mendelssohn ad loc.

208 Ps. 95, 5.

209 Keth. 5a. Cf. J. Sheb. 1, 1 ref. to Lev. 13, 2.

Notice was also taken of disagreement between phrases in a text, thus ויבקע הים was expected instead of ויבקעו המים[210] in agreement with the preceding phrases in the text.[211]

The fact that occasionally a predicate, when preceding more than one subject, agrees in gender and number with the first,[212] was not overlooked. Thus notice is taken of the following: "ותדבר" מרים ואהרן[213] where the predicate is in the fem. sing.;[214] "ויקח" שם ויפת[215] where the predicate is in the sing.;[216] similarly in אז ישיר משה ובני ישראל[217] it is ישיר and not ישירו.[218]

Before concluding this part of our work it may be of interest to record some examples of grammatical terminology employed by the Rabbis.

(a) "לשון זכר" (masculine); "לשון נקבה" (feminine); שיר is לשון זכר, שירה is לשון נקבה and שירות is לשון נקבות[219] (feminine).

(b) "לשון יחידי" (singular); ויאמר is לשון יחידי[220], אותו is a singular form—"אחד ולא שנים",[221] תשחטו is a plural

---

210 Ex. 14, 21.
211 Ex. R. 21, 6. Cf. S. R. Driver on Ex. 14, 21. Cf. infra p. 159 and notes 40-2.
212 Cf. Gesenius K. §146g; M. Mendelssohn on Num. 12, 1.
213 Num. 12, 1.
214 Cf. Sifre ad loc.; Gen. R. 74, 4 ref. to Gen. 31, 14.
215 Gen. 9, 23. Cf. Rashi ad loc.
216 Gen. R. 36, 6. The Tanḥuma distinctly states "it is not written ויקחו but ויקח". The Sept. and Pesh. read here ויקחו.
217 Ex. 15, 1.
218 Ex. R. 23, 9.
219 Ex. R. 23, 11. Cf. Ḳid. 2b and Gen. R. 14, 7.
220 Mak. 23b ref. to 1 Sam. 12, 5.
221 Ḥul. 78b ref. to Lev. 22, 28.

form—"שנים",[222] נפש means "נפש אחת"—one soul—and נפשות means "הרבה נפשות"[223] souls.

(c) "להבא" (future); "לשעבר" (past); יזרע and יעבד[224] are both future (להבא) while נעבד is past (לשעבר).[225]

The foregoing examples of Rabbinic notes on Hebrew grammar may be taken as evidence of their observation of the phenomena of Biblical Hebrew. Some of their terms descriptive of Hebrew grammar, are still in use today in Hebrew treatises on grammar, though, as may be expected, some of their concepts have been modified by modern research. Yet their place in the development of the study of Hebrew grammar cannot be overlooked.

---

222 Ḥul. 82a ref. to Lev. 22, 28.

223 Lev. R. 4, 6 ref. to Gen. 36, 6 and 46, 25.

224 Deut. 21, 4.

225 Soṭa 46b. Cf. Pes. 7a and b ref. to לבער; Gen. R. 22, 5 ref. to Lev. 6, 13.

B. ETYMOLOGY

B. ETYMOLOGY

Rabbinic literature provides many interesting observations on the ORIGIN OF WORDS AND NAMES. In Gen. 5, 29 the name Noah is explained thus: "And He called his name Noah (נח), saying, This same shall comfort us ינחמנו" (i.e., from the word נחם 'comfort'). This explanation of נח from the word נחם—an entirely different stem—is untenable, for as the Rabbis point out, "the name does not correspond to the interpretation (given to it), nor does the interpretation correspond to the name". "It should have said (in the text) either יניחנו[1] 'This same shall give us rest' or 'His name should have been נחמן[2]'". While scholars question[3] the derivation of אשה from איש in Gen. 2, 23—"This shall be called woman because this was taken out of man"—according to the Rabbis it is a PLAY ON WORDS, (לשון נופל על לשון)[4]

---

1 The rendering in Sept. would appear to be based on such a reading.

2 Gen. R. 25, 2. Cf. H. E. Ryle and G. J. Spurrell ad loc.

3 Cf. J.E. vol. 5, p. 276 and H.E. Ryle on Gen. 2, 23. Cf. also J. Hasting, 'The Greater Men and Women of the Bible', London, 1913, vol. 1, p. 5.

4 I. M. Casanowicz, J.E. s.v. 'Alliteration', does not trace this expression further than in Ḳimḥi's Commentary on Micah 1, 10.

based upon the resemblance in sound between the words אשה and איש.[5]

But whilst undoubtedly appreciating its true significance, the Rabbis themselves frequently resort to the Biblical practice,[6] and present a PLAYFUL ETYMOLOGY.

Thus: שטים (Shittim) is associated with the Aramaic word שטא ('folly') "because the Israelites engaged in ways of folly".[7]

רפידים, (Rephidim) is associated with the word רפה ('slacken') "Because there they slackened in (their loyalty to) the Torah".[8]

In contrast with such derivations, which are obviously meant to be playful, in Rabbinic literature many others of MORE SERIOUS IMPORT are found,[9] thus:

5 Gen. R. 31, 8. H. E. Ryle on Gen. 2, 23 observes that "the margin in the E.V. by pointing out that the Hebrew for 'woman' is ISHAH, and for 'man', ISH, shows the resemblance in sound of the two words". See also interesting observation by A. Clarke on the passage.

6 Cf. Gen. 17, 5; 21, 3-6; 32, 29 a.e.

7 Sanh. 106a.

8 Sanh. 106a. For further examples of this kind of playful etymology see the following: אלגביש Ber. 54b; חדקל Ber. 59b; אמן Shab. 119b; אדם Soṭa 5a; איש ואשה Soṭa 17b; אלמנה Keth. 10b; בלעם Sanh. 105a. Not only proper nouns, but other words too, are occasionally treated this way, see Ber. 10b referring to להדפה 2 Kings 4, 27; Ab. Zarah 24b where וישרנה 1 Sam. 6, 12 is connected with שירה.

9 In this connection cf. Appendix, comments on Gen. 14, 13; 18, 25; 23, 9; 32, 24; Ex. 12, 22; 13, 18; Deut. 1, 17b; 6, 7a; 21, 23; Koh. 1, 14.

יורה,[10] ('former rain') from רוה ('saturate') "because it saturates the earth".[11]

אביון, (poor man) from אבה (desire) "because he longs for everything".[12]

עב, (cloud) is derived from the ordinary meaning of the word—viz. 'thick' "since a cloud makes the sky look thick";[13] the clouds are also called שחקים from שחק (grind) because "they grind the water".[14]

כופר, (ransom) from the root כפר (atone).[15]

אברך,[16] from ברך "to bend the knee".[17]

Idols are variously referred to: as מצבה from יצב (stand) "because they are made to stand", as פסל from פסל (to cut) "because they are sculptured" and as מסכה from נסך (cast) "because they are cast".[18]

מפיבושת,[19] taken to be a compound of מפי and בושת i.e., "from my mouth is shame".[20]

---

10 Deut. 11, 14.

11 Taanith 6a. Cf. F. Delitzsch on Prov. 11, 25; Fuerst, s.v. רוה.

12 Lev. R. 34, 6. Cf. Fuerst on those terms.

13 Gen. R. 13, 12.

14 Gen. R. 13, 10. Cf. Dictionaries.

15 Mak. 2b.

16 Gen. 41, 43.

17 Sifre Deut. 1, 1. This is followed by the E.V.; H. E. Ryle; G. J. Spurrell; F. C. Cook. Cf. also J.E. vol. 1, p. 130.

18 Sifra on Lev. 19, 4. Cf. M. Jastrow on those terms.

19 2 Sam. 4, 4.

20 Ber. 4a. Cf. S. R. Driver, on 2 Sam. 4, 4.

בליעל,[21] explained as a compound of בלי and על i.e., "without a yoke".[22]

In a number of instances the meaning of a word is derived from COGNATE LANGUAGES: e.g.,

עויל,[23] is explained to mean "a child" on the analogy of the Arabic "avila".[24]

קשיטה,[25] according to R. Akiba, is derived from the Arabic: "When I visited the coast town I found that they called a meah (a certain coin) 'ḳ'siṭah' ".[26]

יובל, rendered by the E.V. "trumpet", is also in R. Akiba's opinion, derived from Arabic, having the primary significance of "a ram" which stands metonymically for ('ram's horn') קרן היובל.[27]

קבע,[28] is explained from the Arabic as follows: "An

---

21 Deut. 13, 14.

22 Sanh. 113a. Cf. Gesenius K. §81d; G. A. Smith on Deut. 13, 14. The Midrashic etymologies in Gen. R. 42, 5 on the names ברע and ברשע (Gen. 14, 2) agree with S. R. Driver ad loc., and the one given in Sanh. 105a on בלעם agrees with Fuerst s.v. בלעם.

23 Found only in Job 19, 18 and 21, 11, and erroneously rendered by the Versions. Cf. Appendix, comment on Job 21, 11.

24 Gen. R. 36, 1; Lev. R. 5, 1. Cf. A. Cohen, 'Arabism in Rabbinic Literature', J.Q.R., O.S., vol. 3. 1912-13.

25 Occurs only in Gen. 33, 19; Josh. 24, 32 and Job 42, 11.

26 R. Hash. 26a. This interpretation is followed by the E. V. Cf. Gen. R. 79, 7.

27 R. Hash. 26a, followed by Rashi, Ibn Ezra, margin of E. V. and S. R. Driver on Ex. 19, 13; Ḳimḥi on Josh. 6, 5 and Fuerst W. יובל.

28 Mal. 3, 8.

Arabian, when he wishes to say to another, 'Why wilt thou rob me?', expresses himself thus: מה אתה קובעני."[29]

גלמודה,[30] is rendered "lonely" on the analogy of its meaning in Arabic.[31]

יהבך,[32] is explained from the Aramaic meaning of the word, i.e., "burden".[33]

סלסליה,[34] is given the meaning of "turn over"[35] from its use in the current Aramaic vernacular.

אברך,[36] is identified with the title "Alabarchos" in Greek.[37]

An interesting point in philology is mentioned by R. Neḥemiah, who states that the pronoun אנכי is equivalent to the Egyptian pronoun.[38]

---

29 Tanḥ. T'rumah, 9; cf. R. Hash. 26b. This interpretation is followed in the E. V.; cf. F. Delitzsch on Prov. 22, 23. Cf. also J.E. vol. 2, p. 44.

30 Is. 49, 21.

31 Gen. R. 79, 7; cf. R. Hash. 26a; Soṭa 42a.

32 Ps. 55, 23.

33 Gen. R. 79, 7; R. Hash. 26b. This is followed by the E.V. Cf. Ḳimḥi; F. Delitzsch and A. C. Jennings ad loc. all quoting the Rabbis on this text.

34 Prov. 4, 8.

35 Meg. 18a; R. Hash. 28b. This interpretation derives support from the parallelism in the verse. Cf. Fuerst and Fuenn s.v. סלל. In Jerushalmi Soṭa 7, 2 we find the following: "Let not the Syriac (Aramaic) language be despised in thine eyes; for in all three portions of sacred Scripture—in the Torah, the Prophets and the Holy writings—this language is employed", and then the Aramaic fragments in Gen. 31, 47; Jer. 10, 11 and Dan. 2 are quoted. Cf. Appendix, comment on Gen. 31, 47.

36 Gen. 41, 43.

37 Mek. on Deut. 1, 1 quoted in J.E. vol. 6, p. 229 and in Heb. Encyclopedia "Oẓar Yisroel", s.v. Abrech.

38 Cf. Fuerst and W. Wright, 'Comparative Grammar of Semitic Languages', s.v. אנכי.

C. LEXICOLOGY

C. LEXICOLOGY

The Rabbis' concern about Peshaṭ is particularly noticeable in connection with the detailed attention they give to UNUSUAL WORDS, some of them HAPAXLEGOMENA. In some cases it is pointed out that the word is not to be found elsewhere, e.g., in interpreting the word שמיכה[1] to mean "cloth" they point out "We searched the whole Bible and could not find שמיכה as the name of a garment."[2]

The following are examples of Rabbinic interpretations of UNUSUAL WORDS:[3]

נוקד,[4] "shepherd";[5] סגריר,[6] "severe rainstorm";[7] מרחפת,[8]

---

1 Jud. 4, 18.

2 Lev. R. 23, 10. The same kind of remark is to be found in J. Taan. 4, 2; J. Ab. Zarah 1, 1; Sifre on Deut. 1, 1; and in Deut. R. 1, 20 with reference to certain names occurring only once in the Bible, cf. also Gen. R. 78, 14; Num. R. 12, 8.

3 In this connection cf. Appendix, comments on Gen. 14, 1; Ex. 13, 18; Deut. 24, 7.

4 Only twice, in 2 Kings 3, 4 and in Am. 1, 1.

5 Tanḥ. Ki Thisa 5. The Sept. does not appreciate the meaning of the word and merely transliterates it. The Rabbinic interpretation agrees with E. V. and with modern commentators.

6 Only once, in Prov. 27, 15.

7 Yeb. 63b. Cf. F. Delitzsch ad loc. and M. Jastrow s.v. סגריר.

8 Only twice, Gen. 1, 2; Deut. 32, 11.

"hovering";[9] גשיאים,[10] "clouds";[11] תעלה,[12] (lit. channel) means also "mould";[13] תיכונה,[14] "middle", "you cannot say 'middle' (watch), unless there is one before and one after";[15] נשף,[16] "twilight";[17] ותרגנו,[18] denotes "slander";[19] גדידה,[20] "incision"[21] (in the flesh); ראה, דיה and איה,[22] are names for same bird.[23]

Some words or expressions are explained as having a SECONDARY MEANING,[24] thus giving them a wider interpretation than the primary one. For example: ישב, (literally "to sit"), "to stay";[25] יצק, (literally "to pour"),

---

9 Ḥag. 15a. Cf. Appendix, comment on Gen. 1, 2.
10 Ps. 135, 7.
11 Gen. R. 13, 11. Cf. F. Delitzsch ad loc. and Fuerst s.v. נשיא.
12 1 Kings 18, 32.
13 B. Bath. 16a. Vide M. Jastrow s.v. תעלה.
14 Jud. 7, 19.
15 Ber. 3b.
16 1 Sam. 30, 17.
17 Ber. 3b.
18 Deut. 1, 27.
19 Sifre ad loc.; cf. Gen. R. 20, 2; Num. R. 16, 20 tracing נרגן Prov. 16, 28 from רגן. Vide Fuerst s.v. רגן and F. Delitzsch on Prov. 16, 28.
20 Deut. 14, 1.
21 Yeb. 13b; Sifre ad loc.
22 Deut. 14, 13.
23 Ḥul. 63b. Cf. the Sept. and S. R. Driver on the text.
24 In this connection cf. Appendix, comments on Gen. 6, 2; Ex. 1, 8; 1, 8a; 1, 21; 2, 11 and 11a; 2, 25; 13, 12; 22, 7-8; 22, 27; Lev. 18, 21; 19, 4; Num. 3, 10; 5, 17; Deut. 29, 8; 1 Sam. 2, 24.
25 Meg. 21a reconciling Deut. 9, 9 with 10, 10.

"to attend";[26] נטע,[27] and בנה,[28] (literally "to plant" and "to build"), used in the sense of "obtaining";[29] שמים, (lit. "heaven") also means the "upper regions";[30] לעולם,[31] (lit. forever), means also לעולמו של יובל "up to the period of the jubilee";[32] רגלים, from רגל (foot) has the secondary meaning of "times".[33]

The Rabbis anticipated grammarians[34] in calling attention to the fact that in some instances a word may denote a specific idea and yet, in other cases, its opposite, having a POSITIVE and a NEGATIVE meaning. Thus יוסף,[35] denotes "continuation" or "cessation"[36]; דנני,[37] to find guilty"[38] or "to champion one's cause";[39] ועשתה,[40] "to

26 Ber. 7b ref. to 2 Kings 3, 11. This agrees with all commentators ancient and modern. Cf. Targum; Rashi and Ḳimḥi ad loc. Cf. F. C. Cook; C. J. Ellicott ad loc.

27 Deut. 20, 5.

28 Deut. 20, 6.

29 Soṭa 43a and b.

30 Taan. 9b ref. to Deut. 28, 24.

31 Ex. 21, 6.

32 Mek. ad loc. and Ḳid. 15a. Cf. Sifre on Num. 35, 20 that צדיה denotes "laying in wait" i.e., "aim", "intention".

33 Mishnah Ḥag. 1, 1. Cf. A. W. Streane in his translation of Ḥag. 1, 1 note 4 and S. R. Driver on Ex. 23, 14. Cf. S. Rosenblatt, 'Bible Interpretation in the Mishnah', p. 8.

34 Cf. Rashi and M. Mendelssohn on Ex. 27, 3 and Gesenius K. §52h.

35 Gen. 38, 26.

36 Soṭa 10b; cf. Sifre on Num. 11, 25; Sanh. 17a and the Targumim on that text.

37 Gen. 30, 6.

38 As in Gen. 15, 14.

39 As in Deut. 32, 26; cf. Gen. R. 71, 7.

40 Deut. 21, 12.

pare" or "to let grow".[41] Commenting on the AMBIGUITY in the meaning of וחלצה,[42] it is pointed out that חלץ denotes both "loosening" and "girding" but in each case of ambiguity its true implication should be decided by its context.[43]

41 Sifre ad loc.

42 Deut. 25, 9.

43 Yeb. 102b. Cf. Mak. 8a with ref. to AMBIGUITY IN GRAMMAR; Sanh. 4b with ref. to VOCALISATION and B. Meẓ. 56b with ref. to FIGURATIVENESS. See supra p. 110 and note 32.

D. SYNONYMS

D. SYNONYMS

There are several references in Rabbinic literature to, what may loosely be termed, SYNONYMS[1] used in the Bible.

The following are some examples mentioned by the Rabbis:

ניפול, פילול, תחנונים, שועה, צעקה, נאקה, רינה, פגיעה, ביצור, קריאה for prayer;[2]

עב, ענן, אד, נשיאים, חזיז for cloud;[3]

ארץ, תבל, אדמה, ארקא for earth;[4]

נפש, רוח, נשמה for soul,[5]
and in all these cases Biblical verses are quoted to exemplify the use of each synonym.

There are also interesting observations on the DIFFERENT SHADES OF MEANING OF SYNONYMOUS TERMS and, indeed, the Rabbis appear to have appreciated that some of the so-called "synonyms" have the same meaning only in an approximate sense, and differ in some degree.

---

1 In this connection cf. Appendix, comments on Ex. 3, 1a.
2 Deut. R. 2, 1. Cf. Sifre on Deut. 3, 23.
3 J. Taan. 3, 3; cf. Gen. R. 13, 12.
4 Gen. R. 13, 12; Lev. R. 29, 11.
5 Gen. R. 14, 9; Deut. R. 2, 37.

Thus the following distinctions are drawn:

(a) רינה—"Praise of God", תפילה—"praying for one's own needs";[6]

(b) עב—a "heavy" cloud, ענן—a "light" cloud;[7]

(c) אמירה—"gentle speech—distinguished from דבור—"harsh" speech;[8]

(d) חטא, עון and פשע differ in that the first denotes an "inadvertent" act, the second a "wilful" act and the third a "rebellious" act;[9]

(e) ילד—a child of "tender years"—distinguished from נער—an "older child";[10]

(f) אחר—"immediately after" the preceding event (בסמוך)—distinguished from אחרי—a "long time afterwards"[11] (מופלג);

(g) ירה—"cast down"—רמה "thrown up";[12]

(h) קמח—"ordinary meal"—distinguished from סולת—"fine meal"[13]

---

6 Deut. R. 2, 1.

7 Ber. 59a; cf. Malbim on Is. 44, 22 and Fuenn on those words.

8 Mak. 11a a.e.

9 Yoma 36b a.e.

10 Soṭa 12b ref. to Ex. 2, 6.

11 Gen. R. 44, 5. Cf. ibid for a contrary view.

12 Mek. on Ex. 15, 4.

13 B. Meẓ. 87a ref. to Gen. 18, 6. Cf. Appendix, comment on Num. 5, 15.

(i) קידה, כריעה and השתחואה (all of them acts of worship)—the first signifying "falling on the face", the second "kneeling upon the knee", and the third "prostration",[14] spreading out hands and feet;

(j) נגח "goring"—נגף "collision";[15]

(k) אוה "desire" (i.e., merely a state of mind)—distinguished from חמד "covet"[16] (i.e., desire followed by the employment of some means for its attainment);

(l) נטיעה — "planting" — distinguished from שתילה "transplanting".[17]

---

14 Ber. 34b; Meg. 22b; Sheb. 16b.

15 B. Ḳamma 2b ref. to Ex. 21, 28.

16 Mek. on Ex. 20, 14. Cf. M. Mendelssohn on Deut. 5, 18.

17 Ab. Zarah 19a (cf. Rashi ad loc.) ref. to Ps. 1, 3; cf. Malbim on Lev. 19, 23; for another distinction between נטיעה and שתילה cf. Yalḳuṭ on Ps. 1, 3 referred to by F. Delitzsch ad loc. The following words used for different kinds of magic-viz. מכשף, מנחש, מעונן, חובר, קוסם are distinguished. Cf. Sifre on Deut. 18, 10 and 11; Sanh. 65 and 67. Cf. also interesting comments distinguishing שבועת שוא from שבועת שקר, Sheb. 25b; גזל from חמס, B. Ḳamma 62a; עדי from עד, Gen. R. 72, 4; עזיבה from שכיחה, Ber. 32b; חליפה from תמורה, Tem. 9a; צדיק from תמים, Ab. Zarah 6a; פתע from פתאום, Kerith. 9a and Num. R. 10, 13.

PART TWO

THE RABBIS' APPRECIATION OF PESHAṬ

(Continuation)

Metaphors (כביכול, לשכך האזן)

Tikkun Soferim (תקון סופרים)

Euphemism (לישנא מעליא, לשון נקיה)

Hyperbole (לשון הבאי)

Figurative language (משל)

Idiom and Usage (משתעי קרא הכי, אורחיה דקרא הוא)

(דברה תורה כלשון בני אדם)

The Torah employs human language

Scripture speaks of what usually happens (דבר הכתוב בהווה)

Variation in style or deviation from standard literary form

Paralelism

(אין ב' נביאים מתנבאים בסגנון אחד)

Difference in style among the prophets

דברי תורה עניים במקומן ועשירים במקום אחר

Inconsistancies and contradictions

Abbreviation in the text (מקרא קצר)

The wording in the text is to be transposed (מקרא מסורס)

אין מוקדם ומאוחר בתורה

Appendix

PART TWO

CRITICAL ANALYSES OF THE TEXT

The Rabbis' appreciation of Peshaṭ is evidenced not only in the treatment of points of grammar and particular words, but also in many interesting observations displaying a realistic approach.

It is frequently indicated that a particular phrase or expression is not to be taken literally.[1] Whenever actions similar to those of a human being are predicated of God, the Rabbis employ the term כביכול ("as though it were possible")—intending thus to convey that the expressions used are not to be taken literally, but only as METAPHORS, as a mode of speech suited to the average intellect.

The following passage[2] may best illustrate this point. In commenting on the text "And the mount Sinai was . . . as the smoke of a furnace . . .", the Rabbis observe: "One might think that the mountain emitted smoke only like a furnace and not to a greater degree, Scripture therefore states in another passage (Deut. 4, 11) 'And the mountain burned with fire unto the very midst of the heavens'. Then what reason is there for stating that it

1 Cf. M. Gudeman, 'Spirit and letter in Judaism and Christianity', J.Q.R.O.S. vol. 4, 1891-92.

2 Mek. on Ex. 19, 18. Cf. also Mek. on Ex. 15, 17.

smoked only like a furnace? This is said in order to sink into the ear that which it is able to hear (לשכך[3] האוזן מה שהיא יכלה לשמוע), i.e., to assist the perception of man. A similar case is (Hos. 11, 10) 'As a lion does He (God) roar'. But who gave the lion power if not He, and yet Scripture compares Him only to a lion! But the reason is that we describe Him by comparing Him to His creatures (לשכך האוזן). A similar example is, (Ezek. 43, 2) 'And His voice was like the sound of many waters'. But who gave the waters a thunderous sound except He, and yet you describe Him by comparing Him to His handiwork—it is (לשכך האוזן)". The employment of such comparisons relating to God are described by the Rabbis in the following strong terms: "The Prophets show great daring in likening the Creator to the creatures".[4] They also deal with (תיקון סופרים)—EMENDATIONS OR IMPROVEMENT MADE BY THE SCRIBES,[5] i.e., to avoid anthropomorphism and anthropopathism.

Reference is occasionally made to the employment in the Bible of EUPHEMISTIC[6] terms; thus the Rabbis speak of לישנא מעליא ("refined language");[7] לשון נקיה

---

3 Vide Jastrow, s.v. שכך.

4 Gen. R. 27, 1; Ḳoheleth R. 2, 20.

5 For illustrations cf. Mekilta on Ex. 15, 7; Sifre on Num. 10, 35; Gen. R. 49, 7 a.e. Cf. Rashi, English Translation ed. by A. M. Silbermann, on Gen. 18, 22 note 3.

6 Cf. J.E. Vol. 5 s.v. 'Euphemism'.

7 In relation to Gen. 7, 8 cf. Pes. 3a. In relation to Jud. 3, 24; 5, 27; 1 Sam. 24, 4; 2 Sam. 19, 25 cf. Yeb. 103a. In relation to Prov. 30, 20 cf. Keth. 13a. The Sept., Vulg., Targum and margin of the A.V. agree with the Rabbinic renderings of these texts; cf. 'Pulpit Commentary', on 1 Sam. 24, 4.

("decent expression").[8] Similarly, they point to the substitution in Scripture of a modified expression (לשבח) in place of one obscene[9] (לגנאי); e.g., in the reading of the text ישכבנה is to be substituted for the offensive term ישגלנה;[10]
בטחורים for בעפולים;[11]
דביונים for חריונים;[12]
למוצאות for למחראות;[13]
צואתם for חריהם;[14]
מימי רגליהם for שיניהם.[14]

In relation to the use of HYPERBOLICAL language in the Hebrew Bible we find the following: "The Torah speaks in the language of exaggeration and so do the Prophets,"[15] in illustration of which, the following examples are given: "The cities are great and fenced

8 In relation to Gen. 39, 6 cf. Gen. R. 70, 4; cf. Rashi and M. Mendelssohn on Gen. 39, 6.

9 Meg. 25b; Soferim ch. 9.

10 Deut. 28, 30. Cf. Rashi and G. A. Smith on the text. The A. V. agrees with Ḳ're.

11 Deut. 28, 7.

12 2 Kings 6, 25. Cf. Ḳimḥi ad loc.

13 2 Kings 10, 27. Cf. Ḳimḥi ad loc.

14 2 Kings 18, 27. Cf. Ḳimḥi ad loc.

15 Ḥul. 90b; Tem. 29a; Sifre on Deut. 1, 28. The Rabbis likewise frequently employ hyperbolical language, e.g., "Whosoever possesses a presumptuous nature is like one who serves idols" (Soṭa 4b); "He who equivocates in his speech is like an idolater" (Sanh. 92a); "He who does not study deserves to die" (P. Aboth 1, 13). In Ḥul. 90b and Tem. 92a the fact of the use by the early Rabbis of such extravagant modes of expression is specifically noted.

up to heaven";[16] "So that the earth rent with the sound of them".[17]

The attention given by the Rabbis to the use of FIGURATIVE[18] language in the Scriptures is further seen in the following examples: In commenting on the text קח את אהרון ואת בניו[19] the Rabbis, referring also to ויקח משה את האנשים[20] and similar texts, state: "Did Moses really carry people in bundles over his shoulders, but the term קיחה in those cases signifies "winning them over", attracting them by fine words".[21] Again in the comment on Gen. 34, 3 וידבר על לב הנערה (literally "And he spoke to the heart of the damsel") "How can one speak to the heart? It means, he spoke words that would appeal to her heart".[22]

An appreciation by the Rabbis of Biblical IDIOM and USAGE is seen in such an expression as משתעי קרא הכי— "Such is the Scriptural idiom"[23] or אורחיה דקרא הוא—

16 Deut. 1, 28. Maimonides, 'Guide', part 2, ch. 47, must have had another Rabbinic passage in mind; he says: "as a hyperbole our Sages quote (Eccles. 10, 20)".

17 1 Kings 1, 40.

18 In this connection cf. Appendix, comments on Gen. 5, 24; 18, 1; Ex. 17, 11; Lev. 19, 14; Num. 4, 20; 5, 18; Deut. 25, 8; Is. 26, 19.

19 Lev. 8, 2.

20 Num. 1, 17.

21 Sifre on Lev. 8, 2. Cf. Mekilta, Ex. 14, 6; Gen. R. 45, 3; Num. R. 18, 2. Cf. Rashi on Ex. 14, 6; Lev. 8, 2 and on Num. 8, 6.

22 Gen. R. 80, 7. Cf. Rashi Gen. 50, 21. This rendering agrees with the E. V., cf. H. E. Ryle, Gen. 34, 3. Cf. also B. Meẓia 56b ref. to Num. 21, 26.

23 In relation to Gen. 4, 23 and 19, 24 cf. Sanh. 38b; in relation to 1 Kings 1, 33 and Est. 8, 8 cf. Gen. R. 51, 2. Cf. H.E. Ryle on Gen. 19, 24.

"This is the usage of Scripture".[24] It is also pointed out: לשון תורה לעצמה, ולשון בני אדם לעצמן—"Biblical idiom and common parlance (i.e., the later Hebrew) are quite distinct from one another";[25] thus in explaining the word תירוש in Is. 65, 8 it is stated that its meaning in the context is "a berry in the cluster", though in common parlance the word denotes a dried berry.[26]

The Rabbinic statement דברה תורה כלשון בני אדם—"The Torah employs human phraseology", is of considerable importance since it is employed in explaining a number of Biblical usages: (1) the infinitive before a finite verb, e.g., ראה תראה;[27] (2) the repetition of a word, e.g., איש איש;[28] (3) repetition by use of a synonym, e.g., ודבר ואמר.[29] In this connection, reference may also be made to the following Rabbinic canon of interpretation: (דבר הכתוב בהווה) "Scripture (in using certain words) speaks of what usually happens".[30]

With their fluent knowledge of Scripture the Rabbis were quick to seize upon any VARIATION[31] IN STYLE or DEVIATION FROM STANDARD LITERARY

---

24 In relation to Num. 27, 9 cf. B. Bath. 147a.

25 Ḥul. 137b. Ab. Zarah 58b; cf. J. Ned. 6, 1.

26 J. Nazir 2, 1.

27 1 Sam. 1, 11 cf. Ber. 31b.

28 Lev. 22, 4 cf. Yeb. 71a. For the reiteration of a name, cf. Appendix, comment on Ex. 3, 4.

29 Deut. 20, 2-3, see J. Soṭa 8, 1. Cf. J. Yeb. 8, ref. to Gen. 17, 13.

30 Cf. Mekilta on Ex. 22, 30; Sifre on Deut. 23, 11; cf. Rashi on those texts. See also Ḳid. 2b; B. Ḳamma 54b; Sanh. 72b; Bek. 25a. Cf. Appendix, comment on Ex. 22, 17.

31 In this connection cf. Appendix, comment on Gen. 2, 14.

FORM. For example: omission of the words כי טוב in 2 Chron. 20, 11 "Give thanks unto the Lord for His mercy endureth forever";[32] omission of the word ותהר ("and she conceived") in the narrative of Zilpa's childbearing in Gen. 30, 10, contrasted with the usual form of narrative in the case of Jacob's wives[33] ותהר ותלד ("And she conceived and she bore"); omission in 1 Kings 2, 10 and 11, 21 of the title מלך ("King") which usually accompanies the name of David whenever mentioned in the Bible;[34] the order of words in Gen. 2, 4 ("earth and heaven") is contrasted with the usual order of these words, viz. "Heaven and earth";[35] the order in which the names of the daughters of Zelophehad appear in Num. 27, 1 is contrasted with the order given in Num. 36, 11;[36] the term וידבר, found only once in the Book of Joshua[37] in reference to a Divine communication, viz. Josh. 20, 1 ("And the Lord spoke") is contrasted[38] with the usual ויאמר ("And He said"); the term שכב employed in reference to the death of David in 1 Kings 11, 21 is contrasted with the term מת used in the same verse in reference to the death of Joab.[39]

---

32 Sanh. 39b. In this connection cf. Appendix, comment on Gen. 1, 8.

33 Gen. chaps. 29 and 30. Cf. Gen. R. 71, 9.

34 Ḳoh. R. 8, 8.

35 J. Ḥag. 2, 1; Ḥag. 12b. H. E. Ryle and G. J. Spurrell refer to Gen. 2, 4 as an "unusual order of words". Cf. J. H. Hertz and Pulpit Commentary ad loc. A number of illustrations of this kind are given in the last Mishnah of Kerithoth.

36 Sifre on Num. 27, 1.

37 See Rashi on Mak. 11a; Minḥath Shai on Josh. 20, 1.

38 Mak. 11a.

39 B. Bath. 116a.

The Rabbis must have recognised that "The poetical form of the Psalms, as of Hebrew poetry in general, is PARALLELISM".[40] Thus referring to the text "For the Lord hearkeneth unto the needy, and despiseth not His prisoners",[41] they say: "The beginning of this verse does not match its end, nor the end the beginning. The verse should surely have read either, For the Lord . . . the needy . . . the prisoners, or . . . His needy . . . His prisoners".[42]

A point of special interest is the observation of a DIFFERENCE IN STYLE AMONG THE PROPHETS. Thus we are told[43] that "The same communication was revealed to many Prophets, yet no two Prophets prophesy in the identical phraseology". As an example, reference is made to Obad. 1, 3—"The pride of thine heart hath deceived thee", which is compared with the similar context in Jer. 49, 16—"Thy terribleness[44] hath deceived thee, and the pride of thine heart".

In dealing with a particular text the Rabbis draw upon their extensive knowledge of the Scripture as an aid to interpretation.[45] In this connection reference must be

---

40 Cf. M. Friedlander, 'The Jewish Religion', p. 89.

41 Ps. 69, 34.

42 Gen. R. 71, 1. Cf. supra p. 129 and note 211. In this connection, cf. Appendix, comment on Ps. 139, 17.

43 Sanh. 89a.

44 A. W. Streane on this text (Cambridge Bible for Schools) remarks: "The word (terribleness) does not occur elsewhere in the Bible, not even in the corresponding passage of Obadia".

45 In this connection cf. Appendix, comments on Gen. 5, 24; 14, 24; Ex. 21, 15; 22, 12; Deut. 25, 19. Jud. 2, 1; Ps. 51, 19.

made to two interesting Rabbinic statements: "Words of the Torah have need of one another, what the former conceals the latter reveals".[46] Again, "Words of the Torah, though obscure in their own passage, sometimes become clear when enlightened by another passage".[47]

INCONSISTENCIES, expressed or implied, as well as apparent CONTRADICTIONS, are noted by the Rabbis, who seek to reconcile or clarify conflicting passages.[48] The following are some examples of inconsistencies and contradictions discussed:

(a) In their comment on the text[49] ". . . seventy souls of the House of Jacob", they enquire: "Why do you find the number seventy in their total and only seventy minus one in their detailed enumerations?";[50]

(b) The number of Levites given in Num. 3, 39 as 22,000 actually falls short, by 300, of the aggregate of the separate totals mentioned in that chapter;[51]

(c) The period during which the Israelites ate the manna is calculated by the Rabbis in detail and appears to be less, by thirty days, than the full period of forty years mentioned in Ex. 16, 35;[52]

---

46 Num. R. 19, 28. For illustration, cf. ibid. Cf. supra p. 93, note 46.

47 J. R. Hash. 3, 5.

48 In this connection cf. Appendix, comments on Gen. 2, 5;

49 Gen. 46, 27.

18, 5; 33, 14; Ex. 4, 20; 15, 26; Num. 4, 3.

50 B. Bath. 123a.

51 Bek. 5a. Cf. Appendix, comment on Num. 3, 39.

52 Ḳid. 38a.

(d) Similarly the period—forty days—of "spying out" the land of Canaan, mentioned in Num. 13, 25, appears on examination, to fall short, though in this case by one day only;[53]

(e) The period of David's reign over Israel is given in 1 Kings 2, 11 as forty years, but in the light of 2 Sam. 5, 5 the period would appear to be computed as forty years and six months;[54]

(f) From Ex. 17, 5 it is implied that it was Moses who "smote the river", whereas, as stated in Ex. 8, 2 this was done by Aaron;[55]

(g) In 1 Kings 17, 1 Elijah declared that there will be neither "dew nor rain", but the absence of the word "dew" in the later context of 1 Kings 18, 1—"Go show thyself and I will send rain upon the earth" would seem to suggest that only the rain, and not the dew was withheld;[56]

(h) According to verse 18 in Num. 27 it was one hand (ידך "thy hand") only that Moses was to lay on Joshua, whereas according to verse 23 of this chapter he laid both hands [57] (ידיו "his hands");

(i) In Gen. 1, 12 it is stated that at the third day of creation "The earth brought forth grass, herb . . . and tree bearing fruit", but in Gen. 2, 5, dealing with the

53 Taan. 29a.
54 Sanh. 107b.
55 Sanh. 99b.
56 Taan. 3a.
57 B. Ḳamma 92b.

sixth day of creation we find "No shrub of the field . . . and no herb of the field had yet sprung up";[58]

(j) According to Ex. 40, 35 "Moses was not able to enter into the tent of meeting because the cloud abode thereon", while in Ex. 24, 18 it says that "Moses entered into the midst of the cloud";[59]

(k) The period for eating unleavened bread is stated in Deut. 16, 8 to be six days, but in Ex. 12, 15 it is seven days;[60]

(l) The name of the father of Kish is given as Abiel in 1 Sam. 9, 1 and as Ner in 1 Chron. 8, 33.[61]

Sometimes, where modern critics find a corruption in the text, the Rabbis had noted the difficulty and attempted by the use of certain rules, to ascertain the correct meaning. An interesting example of this aspect of Rabbinic exegesis is the employment of the principle of מקרא קצר "ABBREVIATION IN THE TEXT"[62] of which the following illustrations are offered.

(a) 2 Sam. 13, 39 ותכל דוד המלך ("And King David longed"). The use of the feminine prefix in ותכל presents an obvious difficulty; according to the Rabbis the word

---

58 Ḥul. 60b.

59 Yoma 4b. Cf. Sifre on Num. 7, 89 where the apparent contradiction between Ex. 25, 22 and Lev. 1, 1 is reconciled by employing the principle "When two Scriptural verses apparently contradict each other there comes a third and reconciles them".

60 Men. 66a.

61 Lev. R. 9, 2. Cf. Ḳimḥi ad loc.

62 Baraita of R. Eliezer b. Jose ha-Gelili. In this connection cf. Appendix, comments on Num. 35, 33; Deut. 6, 4.

נפש ("Soul") is to be understood and the text is to be interpreted as though it reads thus: ותכל נפש דוד המלך i.e. "and the soul of King David longed".[63]

(b) 1 Chron. 17, 5 ואהיה מאהל אל אהל וממשכן ("I have gone from tent to tent and from tabernacle"). The latter words "and from tabernacle" are unintelligible without some addition to the text;[64] the verse is explained by the Rabbis as though it reads וממשכן למשכן i.e. "and from tabernacle to tabernacle".[65]

Another means employed for arriving at the correct meaning of the text is the Rabbinic formula known as מקרא מסורס — "THE WORDING IN THE TEXT IS TO BE TRANSPOSED"[66] of which the following illustrations are given:

(a) In 1 Sam. 3, 3 ונר אלהים טרם יכבה ושמואל שכב בהיכל ד׳ "And ere the lamp of the Lord went out, and Samuel was lying in the temple of the Lord", the words בהיכל ד׳ ("in the temple of the Lord") clearly cannot be taken in conjunction with 'and Samuel was lying', since one was not allowed to sit down in the

---

63 Baraita ibid. This interpretation agrees with the Targums, Rashi, Ḳimḥi, RaLBaG and the E.V. Cf. also R. P. Smith and S. R. Driver, ad loc. who obtain the same meaning from the reading of the Lucian Recension.

64 C. J. Ball in C. J. Ellicott's ed. of the Commentary of the Bible remarks on this text: "some words must have fallen out".

65 So the Targums, Rashi, Ḳimḥi and the E.V.

66 Baraita of R. Eliezer b. Jose ha-Gelili. But in several instances this device is employed with a view to deriving from the text a homiletical interpretation rather than the plain meaning. Reference is also made to "Misplacement" of words, clauses and sections. Cf. e.g., Shab. 116a; B. Ḳamma 107a, a.e.

temple, much less lie down; they must be transposed, the verse being interpreted thus: "And ere the lamp of the Lord went out in the temple of the Lord and Samuel was laid down".[67]

(b) The context of verse 18 of Ps. 34 should be taken in conjunction with verse 15, the subject of the verb צעקו ("cry") being צדיקים ("righteous") supplied from verse 15.[68] All ancient versions and the E.V. on verse 18 likewise insert "the righteous".

In some cases the Rabbis' treatment of a difficulty in the text is especially interesting because of its DARING MODERNITY. For instance, with reference to Jer. 39, 2 where the date of the breaking-down of the walls of Jerusalem is stated to be the ninth of Tammuz, as opposed to the traditional date recorded in the Mishnah,[69] viz. 17th. Tammuz, we are told:[70] "There is a disarrangement of dates here".[71] The text of Ex. 34, 7 "The Lord is

---

67 Baraita ibid. Cf. also Ḳid. 78b. Commentators agree with the Rabbis that Samuel must have been "sleeping in some chamber near the Ark", J. R. Dummelow. Cf. 'Pulpit Commentary' and S. R. Driver ad loc. This interpretation by way of inversion is followed by Ḳimḥi, Minḥath Shai and the A.V.

68 Baraita ibid. So also Hitzig, Delitzsch, C. A. Briggs and W. E. Barnes. A. Clarke considers that צדיקים ('righteous') "was lost through its similitude to the word צעקו".

69 Taan. 4, 6.

70 J. Taan. 4, 5.

71 According to the Ḳorban HaEdah and Pne Moshe ad loc. it means "that the text records the confused date current among the people". Cf. Taan. 28b where the Rabbis attempted to reconcile the contradiction.

visiting the iniquity of the fathers upon the children" is compared with Ezek. 18, 3: "The soul that sinneth, it shall die", it being stated that Ezekiel revoked the Mosaic pronouncement.[72] This critical approach is also seen in other Rabbinic remarks.[73] Thus: "There is no earlier or later (i.e. no chronological order) in (the events or laws of the) Scripture".[74] The last eight verses of the Pentateuch, according to Rabbi Judah, are from the hand of Joshua.[75] "A certain Rabbi . . . in the course of his expositions remarked, Job never was and never existed, but is only a typical figure".[76] There is also a suggestion[77] that the vision of the Valley of the Dead in Ezekiel (Ch. 37) likewise was a parable. Verses 19 and 20 of Isaiah, chapter 8, are attributed to Beeri (father of Hosea); it is stated that Beeri's prophecies consisted of only two verses, and that insufficient to form a Book in themselves, they were incorporated in the Book of Isaiah.[78]

---

72 Mak. 24a. According to this passage Mosaic pronouncements were also revoked by Amos, Isaiah and Jeremiah, and in all the cases Biblical verses are quoted. Cf. Ber. 7a where Ex. 34, 7 is contrasted with Deut. 24, 16 and reconciled.

73 In this connection cf. Appedix, comments on Gen. 2, 13; 14, 14; Ex. 3, 1.

74 Cf. e.g., J. Meg. 1, 1; Pes. 6b a.e. For interesting illustrations cf. Ḳoh. R. 1, 12. In this connection cf. Appendix, comment on Ex. 20, 15-16.

75 B. Bathra 14b; Men. 30a.

76 B. Bathra 15a.

77 Sanh. 92b.

78 Lev. R. 6, 6. Cf. B. Bathra 14b with reference to the prophecy of Hosea.

APPENDIX

APPENDIX

The quotations cited in this Appendix, set out in chronological order, afford further evidence of the contribution made by the Rabbis to the understanding of the text in its full sense.[1]

The agreement of certain modern scholars with some of the Rabbinic observations may be due to their dependence on the Rabbinic material, either directly from the actual sources of Talmud and Midrash or indirectly through the medium of the mediaeval Jewish exegetes. This theme provides interesting material for study on its own merits[2] and might add force to our argument that Rabbinic exegesis, when separated from purely Midrashic material, possesses a sound and common-sense basis.

Gen. 1, 1: "The heaven and the earth".

"The heaven and the earth, i.e., the universe as it is now, in its complete state", S. R. Driver. This idea, which has been emphasised by both mediaeval and modern commentators, (cf. Maimonides "Guide", part 3, ch. 30, Ḳimḥi in his Book of Roots, s.v. את, M. Mendelssohn, A. Clarke, F. C. Cook, R. P. Smith ed. C. J. Ellicott,

1 At the end of each example reference is made to the appropriate subject matter in the body of the text.

2 Cf. I. Abrahams, 'Rabbinic Aids to Exegesis', in 'Cambridge Biblical Essays', London, 1909.

Pulpit Commentary and J. R. Dummelow ad loc.) is found in *Gen. R. 1, 14:* "R. Ishmael says: 'Eth' (את) is inserted before 'the Heavens' (השמים) to include the sun and moon, the stars and planets; 'We-Eth' (ואת) is inserted before 'the Earth' (הארץ) to include trees, herbage". Cf. supra p. 115 and note 80.

Gen. 1, 2: "And the spirit of God moved (מרחפת)*".*

The Sept. and E. V. render מרחפת "moved"; the margin of R. V. has "was brooding", so J. R. Dummelow. S. R. Driver observes:— "The word occurs besides only in Deut. 32, 11 where it is used of an eagle 'hovering' over its young". This explanation by reference to ירחף in Deut. 32, 11 is also found in *J. Ḥag. 2, 1;* cf. *Ḥag. 15a* and Rashi l.c. As H. E. Ryle points out the rendering "brooding" does not convey the subtle meaning of the word, and he prefers "hovering"; cf. מרחפת in the Rabbinic simile כיונה המרחפת על בניה ואינה נוגעת "like a dove that hovers over her young without touching them", *Ḥag. 15a.* Cf. supra p. 141 and note 8.

Gen. 1, 5: "And God Called the light day, and the darkness He called night".

"God designed the distinction to be permanent", S. R. Driver. This agrees with the Rabbinic interpretation in *Gen. R. 3, 6,* "God called the light (for service by) day, saying to it, 'The day shall be thy province'; And the darkness called He (for service at) night, saying to it, 'Night shall be thy province' ". Cf. *Pes. 2a.* So M. Mendelssohn, J. H. Mecklenburg, and F. Delitzsch quoted in Pulpit Commentary, A. Clarke and C. J. Ellicott, ad loc.

Gen. 1, 8: "And God called the firmament Heaven. And there was evening . . . a second day".

Commentators note the omission of the usual formula "And God saw that it was good" in connection with the second day's work; the addition of it by the Sept. has been questioned, since it had not been acknowledged by any of the Mss. "The explanation of Calvin, Delitzsch, MacDonald . . . is probably the correct one, that the work begun on the second day was not properly terminated till the middle of the third, at which place, accordingly, the expression of Divine approbation is introduced (See ver. 10)", Pulpit Commentary. So A. Clarke, R. P. Smith ed. C. J. Ellicott and S. R. Driver. Similarly the *Midrash questions:* "Why is it not stated in reference to the work of the second day 'that it was good'? R. Samuel said because the work associated with water was not completed until the third day"; therefore the Midrash proceeds:—"on the third day this formula is repeated twice," (*Gen. R. 4, 6*). Cf. supra pp. 157-8 and note 32.

Gen. 2, 5: "And no plant of the field . . . had yet sprung up . . ."

The apparent contradiction between this text and that in Gen. 1, 12 "and the earth brought forth sprouts, herbs . . . and tree . . .", is noted by the *Rabbis* (*Ḥul. 60b*) and explained that "the earth brought forth sprouts, etc." (in Gen. 1, 12) does not signify that they came forth above the ground but that they remained at the opening of the ground (i.e., just below the surface). Cf. supra p. 160 and note 48.

Gen. 2, 13-14: ". . . Cush . . . Asshur . . ."

With reference to the names "Cush" and "Asshur" mentioned in these texts the Rabbis ask (*Keth. 10b and*

Gen. R. 16, 3) "were they already then in existence? But they are mentioned", they say, "because they will exist in the future". Cf. S. R. Driver on Ex. 3, 1 that "the name 'Mountain of God' is so called proleptically". According to *R. Joseph* (*Keth. ibid*) Asshur is the name of a city and not of the whole land of Assyria, cf. H. E. Ryle ad loc. Cf. infra comment on Gen. 14, 14. Cf. supra p. 165 note 73.

Gen. 2, 14: "And the fourth river is the Euphrates".

Since no further description is given of this river, as in the case of the other three rivers mentioned, commentators observe that "the Israelites seem to have regarded the Euphrates as 'the river par excellence' ", H. E. Ryle; cf. also Pulpit Commentary. This agrees with *Rab's statement, in Bek. 55b,* that Euphrates is superior to all the other rivers, see Gen. 15, 18; Deut. 1, 7 referring to Euphrates as "the great river", cf. J. H. Hertz ad loc. On the other hand *Simeon b. Tarfon, in Sheb. 47b,* seems to differ on this point. Referring to Deut. 1, 7 "As far as the great river, the river Euphrates", he says: "go near a fat man, and be fat" and "in the school of R. Ishmael it was taught: The servant of a King is like a King", (i.e., "the river Euphrates is not really greater, but smaller, than the others, for it is mentioned last of the four rivers in Gen. 2, 14, but it is called in Deut. 1, 7 'the great river', because it is mentioned in connection with the Land of Israel and anything connected with the Holy Land is great", Rashi ad loc.). Cf. supra p. 157 note 31.

Gen. 2, 15: "To dress it and to keep it".

"The Lord God puts man into the garden for a life, not of indolence, but of labour", H. E. Ryle. The same idea is conveyed in *Aboth di Rabbi Nathan ch. 11.* Thus it says: "See what a great thing is work! The first man was not to taste of anything until he had done some work. Only after God told him to cultivate and keep the garden, did He give him permission to eat of its fruits".

Gen. 3, 12: "The woman whom thou gavest to be with me".

The words 'whom thou gavest to me' suggest, according to the Rabbis (*Ab. Zarah 5b*) ingratitude and an attempt to exculpate himself by throwing responsibility upon God who had given him the woman. Cf. Pulpit Commentary, A. Clarke, H. E. Ryle, M. Mendelssohn and J. H. Hertz.

Gen. 3, 21: "And the Lord God made for Adam . . . coats of skins".

H. E. Ryle draws attention to the "Divine act of pity" in this text. The same idea is expressed by *the Rabbis* (*Soṭa 14a*) thus: "Torah begins with 'an act of benevolence . . . for it is written, And the Lord God made for Adam . . . coats of skins".

Gen. 4, 1: קניתי איש את ד' *"I have gotten a man* את ד'".

Targ. Onk. (so A.V.) renders את "from" i.e., as a gift from the Lord. Most of the modern commentators, however, take את as a preposition meaning "with" in the sense given by the Sept., and R. V. ("with the help of") ; cf. the *Rabbinic* interpretation: "She meant to say:— 'when He created me and my husband He created us by Himself, but in the case of this one (Cain) we are co-partners 'with' Him", (*Gen. R. 22, 2*) ; cf. also *Nid. 31a.* Cf. supra p. 115 and note 82.

Gen. 4 4: "ומחלביהן".

Two different interpretations are given by the *Rabbis (Zeb. 116a)*.

1. The 'fat pieces' of the firstlings.

2. The 'fatlings' of the firstlings.

The rendering by the E. V. "of the fat thereof" agrees with the first interpretation, and literally as taken by the Pulpit Commentary, it agrees with the second interpretation which is the one adopted by the Sept. Cf. supra p. 98 note 78.

Gen. 5, 24: "And Enoch walked with God; and he was not, for God (לקח אותו) *took him".*

A whole circle of apocalyptic literature was ascribed to Enoch. Several commentators, following Sept. and Vulg. are satisfied with the meaning of these words as given by the New Testament, Heb. 11, 5 viz. that Enoch never died. Cf. G. J. Spurrell, F. C. Cook and J. R. Dummelow. It is even argued that otherwise the term וימת instead of לקח would be expected. The *Rabbis (Gen. R. 25, 1)* however, understanding the expression לקח as a figure of speech, accept the plain meaning of the text: namely that he died, on the analogy of the use of the same expression in Ezek. 24, 16; cf. Rashi, Ibn Ezra and M Mendelssohn ad loc. Cf. supra pp. 156 and note 18; 159-160 and note 45.

Gen. 6, 2: בני האלהים *"The sons of God".*

Some commentators, as well as the E.V., render the term "Elohim" in this text in its literal sense. F. C. Cook, G. J. Spurrell and others, however, understand בני האלהים

in the secondary sense as referring to the sons of "nobles". This interpretation is first given by R. Simon b. Joḥai *(Gen. R. 26, 5)* and is followed by the Targums, Rashi, Ibn Ezra, RaMBaN and M. Mendelssohn ad loc. Cf. supra p. 142 and note 24.

Gen. 7, 22: מכל אשר בחרבה מתו *"of all that was in the dry land died".*

"As if to emphasise the thought that the marine animals survived," H. E. Ryle. Cf. Rashi, M. Mendelssohn and the Pulpit Commentary ad loc. So the *Rabbis (Ḳid. 13a; cf. Sanh. 108a; Zeb. 113b)* laying stress upon the term בחרבה remark "but not the fish in the sea".

Gen. 10, 12: "And Resen between Nineveh and Calah the same is the great city".

According to *the Rabbis (Yoma 10a)* it is not clear whether it is to Resen or to Nineveh that the latter part of the text refers. *The Rabbinic view (ibid),* that it refers to Nineveh, was adopted by most commentators. Cf. Ibn Ezra, M. Mendelssohn, F. C. Cook, Pulpit Commentary, Skinner, H. E. Ryle and J. H. Hertz. Cf. supra p. 98 and note 78.

Gen. 12 3: "And in thee shall all the families of the earth be blessed".

Rashi, and after him some moderns, interpret the Niph'al ונברכו in a reflexive sense: "shall bless themselves" while the Versions: Sept., Onk., Vulg., followed by the E.V., render in the passive "shall be blessed", understanding the word בך as meaning "through thee", "on account of thee". Similarly the Rabbinic interpretation in *Gen. R. 39, 12:* "בך—this means, for thy sake", thus the meaning of the text: 'on account of thee the whole world shall be blessed'; cf. Yeb. 63a. Cf. H. E. Ryle and G. J. Spurrell ad loc. Cf. supra pp. 119-120 and note 98.

Gen. 14, 1: "Tidal king of Goiim".

The term גויים is rendered by the Targums as "nations"; so A.V. and R.V. marg.; while the Midrash, *(Gen. R. 42, 4)* followed by Rashi, understands the word as a proper name (as found in Josh. 12, 23); so R.V., cf. H. E. Ryle ad loc. Cf. supra p. 141 and note 3.

Gen. 14, 2: "Bera King of Sodom, Birsha King of Gomorrah".

"Bera and Birsha may be intended by the writer to suggest the meaning with evil (ברע) and with wickedness (ברשע)", S. R. Driver. Cf. *Gen. R. 42, 5,* where R. Joshua explains these names as being compounds viz. "Bera signifies that he was an evil son (ben ra); Birsha that he was a wicked son (בן רשע)", this is followed by Gesenius, Heb. and Chal. Lex. s.v.; cf. infra on Ex. 2, 18. Cf. supra p. 122 and note 123.

Gen. 14, 4: "Twelve years they served Chedorlaomer, and in the thirteenth (ושלש עשרה) *year they rebelled".*

R. Jose (*Gen. R. 42, 6*) *and Rab* (*Shab. 11a*), *followed* by Targ. Onk. and Rashi, take the words ושלש עשרה literally: "and thirteen years"; while R. Simeon b. Gamliel (*Gen. R. ibid*) after him, Targ. Jon. and E. V., render :"and in the thirteenth year"; cf. the rendering ובשלש instead ושלש in the Sam.; cf. Gesenius K. § 134[o]. Cf. supra p. 114 and note 78.

Gen. 14, 13: "Abraham the Hebrew".

Until recent times scholars were divided as to the origin of the name "Hebrew". Either the word עברי is a patronymic from עבר (cf. Gen. 10, 21; 11, 16) and signifies a descendant of "Eber"; or it means "one from the other side" (cf. Josh. 24, 3). Cf. H. E. Ryle, F. C. Cook, Pulpit Commentary and S. R. Driver ad loc. Both views are to be found in *Gen. R. 42, 8:*— "according to R. Neḥemiah (the word Ha-Ibri denotes that) he was descended from Eber, but according to the traditional interpretation (the meaning is that) he came from across the river". Cf. supra p. 134 note 9.

Gen. 14, 14: "And pursued as far as Dan".

There is a difficulty connected with the name Dan mentioned here, since the name was given to the place (formerly Laish) after its capture by the Danites. The Pulpit Commentary, Ewald, and H. E. Ryle treat the reference to "Dan" as an interpolation. According to the Rabbis (*Gen. R. 43, 2*) Dan in this context "is the name of a certain idol". This agrees with the view of "Kuenen and others after him, such as Cheyne, who argue that Dan is the title of a deity", J.E., vol. 4, p. 423. Cf. *Shab. 67b.* See M. Mendelssohn ad loc. Cf. supra p. 165 and note 73.

Gen. 14, 24: ". . . the men which went with me: Anner, Eschol, and Mamre, let them take their portion".

"The rule, laid down by David, 1 Sam. 30, 24-5, for the division of the spoil between combatants and non-combatants was an ancient one. See Num. 31, 27; and cf. Josh. 22, 8. David enforced a special application of it with reference to the divisions of the army", Kirkpatrick, 1 Sam. 30, 24, Cambridge Bible for Schools. The Rabbis similarly observed that David's act, in dividing the spoil equally, was based on the precedent of Abraham in this text, (*Gen. R. 43, 9*). Cf. supra pp. 159-160 and note 45.

Gen. 18, 1: כחם היום *". . . in the heat of the day".*

This phrase is the subject of Midrashic interpretations (*cf. B. Meẓ. 86b*); even the literal exegete RaSHBaM, and F. C. Cook find in it deeper implications. But in *Ber. 27a and in Gen. R. 48, 8* the phrase is interpreted as a figure of speech as the description of the hour in the day viz. "the sixth hour", which agrees with the rendering of the Sept. "noon time"; cf. Mendelssohn, the Pulpit Commentary and H. E. Ryle ad loc. Cf. supra p. 156 and note 18.

Gen. 18, 3: "And said אדני*".*

Some *Rabbis (Sheb. 35b),* followed by Sept., Targums, and the Massoretic text, render it "O Lord" as addressed to God; so R. V. marg. Other *Rabbis (Sheb. ibid and Gen. R. 48, 10*) on the other hand, render it 'My lord' as addressed to the one who appeared to be the chief of the three men. This agrees with the E. V. and with all moderns; cf. M. Mendelssohn, F. C. Cook, H. E. Ryle and J. H. Hertz ad loc. Cf. supra p. 98 and note 78.

Gen. 18, 5: "And I will fetch a morsel of bread".

According to vv. 7-8, however, Abraham fetched a calf, butter and milk and set it before them. "A modest way of describing the rich meal he will set before them", Dillmann. Cf. the *Rabbinic remark, in B. Meẓ. 87a,* on this verse: "It is a mark of the good man, to perform more than he promises"; cf. F. C. Cook, the Pulpit Commentary and H. E. Ryle.

Gen. 18, 25: "חלילה לך".

The *Rabbis in Ab. Zarah 4a,* commenting on this text say: "What Abraham said is: Sovereign of the Universe, it is profanation to do after this manner", connecting, thereby, the word חלילה with חול profane, as secondary root of חלל. This agrees with Targ. Jon., followed by Rashi, M. Mendelssohn, G. J. Spurrell, and Pulpit Commentary; cf. also Fuerst and Talmud Soncino Press, ad loc. Cf. supra p. 134 and note 9.

Gen. 23, 9: ". . . the cave of Machpelah".

The Rabbinic explanation *(Erub. 53a),* of the name מכפלה as a derivative from כפל "double", agrees with all the ancient Versions. Cf. Pulpit Commentary, H. E. Ryle and M. Mendelssohn ad loc. Cf. supra p. 134 and note 9.

Gen. 28, 13: "And behold the Lord stood (עליו)".

There is uncertainty about the meaning of עליו as it may be taken as referring either to the ladder (so the ancient Versions followed by E. V.—'above it') or to Jacob (so Rashi, R. V. marg. and modern commentators; cf. H. E. Ryle and J. H. Hertz — 'beside him'). Both interpretations are recorded in *Gen. R. 69, 3.* Cf. supra p. 98 and note 78.

Gen. 31, 47: "And Laban called it Jegar-sahadutha: but Jacob called it Galeed".

The Rabbis point out in various passages that Jegar-Sahadutha is the Aramaic equivalent for the Hebrew Galeed (*See Shab. 115b. Meg. 9a and J. Soṭa 7, 7*). Cf. supra p. 137 and note 35.

Gen. 31, 52: "That I will not pass over this heap to thee, and that thou shalt not pass over this heap . . . unto me (לרעה)".

At first sight this text does not lend itself to literal translation namely that Laban and Jacob bound themselves never to pass the heap. Some (e.g., Ibn Ezra and A. L. Gordon) interpret the words אעבור and תעבור in the sense of "transgressing" the covenant made at the heap. The Rabbis, however, render them literally, "to pass", but go on to explain that the text should be arranged thus: thou shalt not pass over — this heap and this pillar unto me — for harm, thus stressing that the covenant was only against "passing over" the heap "for evil" (לרעה) but not against passing over for legitimate purposes, *Gen. R. 74, 15.* Cf. Pulpit Commentary ad loc. Cf. supra p. 97 and note 67.

Gen. 32, 24: ". . . and there wrestled (ויאבק) *a man".*

The word ויאבק rendered by the E. V. "wrestled", has been given by the Rabbis *(Ḥul. 91a),* two different renderings.

1. As a denominative form of אבק "dust", i.e., the dust that wrestlers usually raise in the course of wrestling.

2. As a weakened form of חבק "to fold round", "for such is the manner of two people who endeavour to throw each other that they embrace one another", Rashi, Gen. 32, 24. The first rendering is adopted by the Midrash (*Gen. R. 77, 3*), Ibn Ezra, Ḳimḥi Shroshim s.v. אבק and Gesenius, while Fuerst gives the second rendering. Cf. supra p. 134 and note 9.

Gen. 33, 14: "Until I come unto my lord to Seir".

Modern commentators note that although the appointed place of meeting was at Seir, Scripture records (Gen. 33, 17) that Jacob proceeded only as far as Succoth, which is before Seir. Cf. A. Clarke, R. P. Smith and H. E. Ryle who do not question the sincerity of Jacob's promise but explain that he was unable to carry it out. Perhaps a simpler explanation is that given by the Rabbis in *Ab. Zarah 25b:* "If the heathen asks the Israelite whither he is going, he should say towards a place beyond his actual destination (the heathen may then defer the carrying out of his contemplated attack), 'Just as our father Jacob acted towards the wicked Essau', for Scripture says, 'Until I come to my lord to Seir' (Gen. 33, 14), while it records, 'And Jacob journeyed to Succoth' (Gen. 33, 17)". Cf. supra p. 160 and note 48.

Gen. 47, 31a: "וישתחו ישראל על ראש המטה".

The word וישתחו is usually explained by commentators as signifying an act of worship and thanksgiving by Jacob to God for the promise made to him by Joseph; cf. F. C. Cook and H. E. Ryle ad loc. So the Vulg. and other Versions. On the other hand, in *Meg. 16b* the view is expressed that Jacob plainly bowed as a mark of homage to Joseph, who was of higher rank, thus rendering וישתחו "bowed himself" which is followed by the E. V. Cf. supra p. 98 and note 78.

Gen. 47, 31b: "על ראש המטה".

The Sept., Pesh. and likewise Heb. 11, 21 have ". . . leaning upon the top of his staff", vocalising הַמַּטֶּה for הַמִּטָּה. The E.V. and most modern commentators follow the Rabbinic vocalisation הַמִּטָּה — "bed" found in *Shab. 10a; Meg. 16b, and Ned. 40b*. Cf. supra p. 110 and note 28.

Ex. 1, 8: "Now there arose a new King".

The peculiarity of the phrase "a new King", which is not found elsewhere, is explained by one Rabbi *(Soṭa 11a)* as implying the rise of a new policy. Cf. F. C. Cook, A. H. McNeile and S. R. Driver. Cf. supra p. 124 and note 24.

Ex. 1, 8a: אשר לא ידע את יוסף *"Who knew not Joseph".*

"Not only literally, was not acquainted with Joseph, but also, it is implied, did not remember his (Joseph's) services to Egypt, and had no . . . care for his people", S. R. Driver. This form of rendering ידע in its secondary sense agrees with the Rabbinic remark (*Soṭa 11a*) that Pharaoh "appeared like one who did not know him (Joseph) at all". A. Clarke rightly observes "the verb ידע, which we translate to know, often signifies to acknowledge". Cf. supra p. 124 and note 24.

Ex. 1, 15: "And the King of Egypt spoke למילדות העבריות".

Sept., followed by Josephus, renders "to the midwives of the Hebrews", i.e., in the construct, Egyptian women who served as midwives to the Hebrews. Cf. F. C. Cook and A. H. McNeile ad loc. The E. V., followed by A. Clarke and S. R. Driver, however, agree with the Rabbis (*Ex. R. 1, 14; Soṭa 11b*) that the midwives were Hebrews, rendering in the absolute thus: "to the Hebrew midwives". "The Hebrew construction admits of either rendering", C. J. Ellicott ad loc. Cf. supra p. 114 and note 75.

Ex. 1, 21: "... He made them (להם) *houses".*

Mendelssohn and other commentators take להם as referring to the people of Israel, and A. Clarke supports this view from the fact that the pronoun is in the masculine gender. The Rabbis, however, understood it as referring to the midwives, i.e., as a reward God blessed them with marriage and descendants of higher rank, the word בתים being taken in a wider sense to mean "dynasties", (*Ex. R. 1, 17; Soṭa 11b*). This interpretation is followed by Rashi, Ibn Ezra, S. R. Driver, A. H. McNeile and J. R. Dummelow. As for the use of the masculine gender, cf. A. H. McNeile: ". . . but that is found not infrequently with feminine nouns in the plural". Cf. supra p. 142 and note 24.

Ex. 2, 11: "And it came to pass in those days, when Moses was 'grown up' (ויגדל) *that he went out unto his brethren, and 'looked' on their burdens; and he saw an 'Egyptian' smiting an Hebrew".*

"The word for grown up is the same as in V.10, but with a somewhat different force", A. H. McNeile l.c. "Literally, when Moses became great", J. H. Hertz. The *Rabbis,* commenting on this verse, ask: "Has it not already been written (v. 10) 'and the child grew?' *R. Judah said:* 'The first time it refers to growth in stature, the second time to greatness", thus ויגדל is taken here in its secondary sense meaning 'became great', *Yalkuṭ end* § 166. Cf. supra p. 142 and note 24.

Ex. 2, 11a: "And looked on".

"I.e., contemplated with sympathy or grief. More than merely 'saw' ", S. R. Driver. "To look at with pain or *emotion"*, J. Fuerst s.v. ידע. The Rabbis understanding וירא in its deeper implication observe:—"What is the meaning of 'and he looked'? He looked upon their burdens and wept", (*Ex. R. 1, 27*). Cf. supra p. 142 and note 24.

Ex. 2, 11b: "An Egyptian".

"Perhaps one of the 'task-masters', or superintendents of the labour-gangs", S. R. Driver. Cf. also F. C. Cook. The Rabbis (Ex. R. 1, 28) in picturing the cruel manner in which the Egyptian task-masters treated the Israelites, (in course of which distinction is made between נוגש and שוטר), refer to the Egyptian, in the text under consideration, as נוגש מצרי "an Egyptian task-master".

Ex. 2, 14: "Surely the thing is known".

Commenting on this text the *Rabbis* (*Ex. R. 1, 29*) observe that here Moses finds the answer to his question "what has Israel done to deserve such wretchedness". שלא נשמע הדבר אלא על ידי העברים, "The thing (the slaying of the Egyptian) was only heard of through the Hebrews". "It is characteristic", observes Stanley, "of the faithfulness of the sacred records that his (Moses') flight is occasioned rather by malignity of his countrymen than by the enmity of the Egyptians", Hist. of the Jewish Church, vol. 1, lect. 5.

Ex. 2, 18: "And when they came unto Reuel their father".

"Heb. רעואל the 'friend' or 'companion of God' ", S. R. Driver. Similarly, the Rabbis comment: "Why was his name called Reuel? Because he became a friend of God", (*Ex. R. 1, 32*) thus taking Reuel as a compound, רע-אל. Cf. supra p. 122 and note 124.

Ex. 2, 25: "And God saw (וידע) *the children of Israel* (וירא) *and God took knowledge of them".*

" 'Saw', viz. with attention and sympathy. 'Took knowledge', lit. knew them, i.e., noticed, regarded them", S. R. Driver. These ideas are already expressed by the Rabbis in *Ex. R. 1, 35:* "And (God) saw—even as it says (3, 7) 'I have surely seen the affliction of my people' and (God) knew, even as it says (3, 7) 'for I know their sorrow' ", thus, taking the text in its wider implications. Cf. supra p. 142 and note 24.

Ex. 3, 1: "And he came to the mountain of God unto Horeb".

Referring to the expression "mountain of God", S. R. Driver remarks: "It is possibly so called proleptically, in virtue of the sanctity acquired by it from the subsequent law-giving"; cf. the Rabbinic interpretation in *Ex. R. 2, 4:* "The name 'mountain of God' was given because it was there that Israel accepted the Godhead of the Holy One, blessed be He". Cf. Rashi and Mendelssohn ad loc. Cf. supra p. 165 and note 73.

Ex. 3, 1a: "Horeb".

Refering to the two names, "Horeb" and "Sinai", S. R. Driver remarks: "They are almost interchangeable; both denote the mountain of the law-giving". This is in accordance with *Ex. R. 2, 4; 51, 8* and *Shab. 89a.* Cf. supra p. 147 and note 1.

Ex. 3, 4: "Mose, Moses".

R. Simeon b. Joḥai says: "The repetition of the name is an expression of affection intended to encourage him", *Ex. R. 2, 6;* cf. Mendelssohn; A. L. Gordon and

S. R. Driver ad loc. See also H. E. Ryle on Gen. 22, 11 and Gen. R. 56, 7. Cf. supra p. 157 and note 28.

Ex. 4, 20: "And Moses took his wife and his sons".

"The birth of only one son has been hitherto mentioned (Ex. 2, 22). Dillman and others are therefore probably right in thinking that we should read his "son", the plural being an alteration", S. R. Driver; so A. H. McNeile. The Rabbis, however, distinctly say that verse 25 refers to the circumcision of Eliezer, his second son, so that at the time of his departure from Egypt he had already two 'sons', (*Ex. R. 5, 8*). "It is very likely", observes A. Clarke, "that these two sons were born within a short space of each other"; cf. Ibn Ezra, Mendelssohn and S. L. Gordon ad loc. The Sept., Vulg., Syriac, Coptic, and the Arabic, add to Ex. 2, 22 "And the name of the second he called Eliezer". Cf. supra p. 160 and note 48.

Ex. 11, 4: "כחצות הלילה".

Commentators argue whether כחצות is an infinitive with prefix i.e., "when the night is divided", or is another form of the noun חצי with preposition, when the rendering would be "about midnight". The latter is in accordance with the *Rabbinic interpretation* (*Ber. 3b*) and is adopted by Ibn Ezra, the E. V., S. R. Driver, J. R. Dummelow and others; cf. Rashi, RaSHBaM and Mendelssohn. Cf. supra p. 112 and note 50.

Ex. 12, 22: "בסף".

R. Ishmael, in Mek. ad loc. renders בסף "threshold" comparing it with הספום Is. 6, 4 and ספום Ezek. 43, 8; so the Sept. and the Vulg. *Rabbi Akiba* (ibid) however, renders "bason" on the analogy of הספות in 1 Kings 7, 3;

so the E. V. and A. H. McNeile. Cf. *J. Pes. 9, 5.* Cf. supra p. 134 and note 9.

Ex. 13, 10: "Thou shalt therefore keep this ordinance in its season from year to year (מימים ימימה)."

This termination ָה in ימימה is explained by the Rabbis as meaning "from year to year", *Men. 36b;* so Targ. Onk., E. V., S. R. Driver and many other commentators. Cf. Gesenius K. §90h. Cf. supra p. 116, note 91.

Ex. 13, 12: "והעברת כל פטר רחם".

"The word (והעברת) is not the ordinary Hebrew for 'set apart'; and its use here is remarkable", S. R. Driver. F. C. Cook remarks: "Lit. as in the margin 'cause to pass over', but the sense is correctly expressed in the text, which follows the Old Versions and is preferable to the marginal rendering". So E. V. The Rabbis likewise, not taking the word in its ordinary sense, emphasise that והעברת in this text must mean "setting apart" (*Mekilta l. c.*). Cf. supra p. 142 and note 24.

Ex. 13, 18: "And the children of Israel went up armed".

The Rabbinic rendering of this rare expression (וחמֻשים) "provided with weapons", (*Ex. R. 20, 19, and Mek. ad loc.*) is followed by Targ. Onk., Ḳimḥi and E.V.; cf. S. R. Driver. "The objection that the Israelites were not likely to have been armed is unreasonable", A. Clarke. A. H. McNeile's suggestion of connecting the expression וחמשים with the numeral five is also found in the Mekilta l.c.; cf. Ewald, and Keil on Josh. 1, 14. Cf. supra pp. 134 and note 9; 141 and note 3.

Ex. 17, 11: "And it came to pass, when Moses held up his hand, that Israel prevailed; and when he let down his hand, Amalek prevailed".

"A gesture suggestive partly of strenuousness and energy, partly of appeal to God", S. R. Driver. "The scene has often been regarded as typical of the power of prayer", A. H. McNeile. "We cannot understand this transaction in any literal way; for the lifting up or letting down the hands of Moses could not, humanly speaking, influence the battle . . . it is likely that by this act prayer and supplication are intended", A. Clarke. Cf. also F. C. Cook. So too, the *Rabbis observe:* וכי ידיו של משה עושות מלחמה "But could Moses' hands win the battle?" The explanation is given there that "the Israelites were inspired with courage when they saw Moses' hands raised heavenwards in prayer to God", *R. Hash. 29a; and Mekilta l.c.* Cf. G. Margoliouth, 'Moses at the Battle of Rephidim', 'The Expositor' 5th Series No. 26. Cf. supra p. 156 and note 18.

Ex. 18, 21: "Rulers of thousands . . . fifties . . . tens".

"The elaborate organization . . . is an ideal never reached in any nation . . . if Israel numbered 600,000 the required number of rulers would be 78,600", A. H. McNeile. This was already stated by the Rabbis. Commenting on this text they observe:— "Hence the total number of Judges in Israel was 78,600", (Mek. ad loc.; Sanh. 18a). Cf. Talmud, 'The Soncino Press', note 11 ad loc.

Ex. 20, 15-16: "And all the people saw the thunderings . . . And they said unto Moses, speak thou".

According to modern scholars, this phenomenon, though recorded after the revelation of the Decalogue, in fact preceded it in point of time, cf. A. H. McNeile Ex. 19, 19. The same view is taken by the Rabbis in *Ber. 6b,* see also RaMBaN ad loc. Cf. supra p. 165 and note 74.

Ex. 21, 15: "ומכה אביו ואמו מות יומת".

The Rabbis (*Sanh. 84b*) commenting on this text observe: "Since it is written (Ex. 21, 12) 'He that smiteth a man, so that he dies . . .' and also (Num. 35, 21) 'or in enmity smite him . . .that he die', it follows that whenever an unqualified smiting (הכאה) is mentioned (in the Torah) it does not mean slaying", thus he who strikes his Father or Mother is subject to the death penalty. Cf. supra pp. 159-160 and note 45.

Ex. 22, 7-8: "עד האלהים . . . ונקרב . . . אל האלהים".

The term אלהים in these texts rendered by the R. V. "God", is interpreted by the Rabbis (*Sanh. 3b*) in its secondary sense to mean "Judges"; so A.V. and the R.V. marg. Cf. supra observation on Gen. 6, 2, in this Appendix. Cf. supra p. 142 and note 24.

Ex. 22, 12: "If it be torn in pieces, let him bring it for witness".

The uncertainty about the meaning of this text gave rise to several interpretations of יביאהו עד in *Mekilta* (l. c.) of which two are here noted:

(1) "Let him bring witnesses"—the suffix הו in יביאהו being apparently taken by *Mekilta* as anticipating the accusative עד as in ותראהו את הילד ("she saw him, viz. the child") in Ex. 2, 6. This particular interpretation is followed by Targ. Onk. and adopted by Rashi.

(2) "Let him bring it for witness", the suffix הו being taken to refer to the torn animal. In support of this inter-

pretation *Mekilta* refers to Am. 3, 12: "As the shepherd taketh out of the mouth of the lion two legs, or piece of an ear". So Targ. Jon. and Targ. Jerushalmi: "Bring the torn flesh as evidence" and E. V. "Bring it", and also RaSHBaM, Ibn Ezra, A. Clarke, F. C. Cook, A. H. McNeile, S. R. Driver and many other modern commentators; cf. *B. Ḳamma 10a.* Cf. supra p. 98 note 78 and pp. 159-160 and note 45.

Ex. 22, 17: "Thou shalt not suffer a sorceress (מכשפה) ***to live".***

מכשפה "The use of the fem. form can only be accounted for by supposing that, practically, witchcraft was at the time mainly professed by females", Ellicott. Similarly the Rabbis explain (*Sanh. 67a*) that "Scripture speaks of what is usually the case". Cf. S. R. Driver. Cf. supra p. 157 and note 30.

Ex. 22, 27: "אלהים לא תקלל".

Two interpretations are given by different Rabbis (***Mek. ad loc. and Sanh. 66a***).

(1) אלהים is to be taken in its primary sense of "God" i.e., a prohibition of blasphemy; so E. V. and best modern authorities; cf. A. Clarke and F. C. Cook ad loc.

(2) אלהים is to be taken in its secondary sense of "Judge" (as in Ex. 22, 7), i.e., prohibition against cursing a Judge; so Targums, Ibn Ezra, RaSHBaM and margin of the E.V. Cf. supra p. 142 and note 24; p. 98 and note 78.

Lev. 18, 21: "And thou shalt not give any of thy seed . . . to Molech".

This text is rendered by Targ. Jon. as well as by the school of *R. Ishmael:* "Thou shalt not give of thy seed in sexual intercourse to a heathen woman to beget children for idolatry", *Meg. 25a.* The *Mishnah* (*Meg. 4, 9*), however, distinctly emphasises that the text is to be taken literally, i.e., "Thou shalt not give any of thy seed to make them pass through the fire to Molech". So *Talmud Sanh. 64b.* Cf. A. Clarke, F. C. Cook and J. H. Hertz ad loc. Cf. supra p. 142 and note 24; and p. 87.

Lev. 18, 24: "Defile not ye yourselves in 'any' of these things (בכל אלה)*: for in 'all' these* (בכל אלה)".

E. V., followed by all modern commentators, take (בכל) in the first part of the verse distributively ("any") and in the second part collectively ("all"). This agrees with *R. Akiba's remark:*—"Is the prohibition against all combined only, but not against one? Surely not! But it means in one of these things באחת מכל אלה", (Sanh. 81a. Cf. Sifra l. c.). Cf. Gesenius K. §123c. Cf. supra p. 112 and note 55.

Lev. 19, 4: "Turn ye not unto idols".

According to the prevailing view among the *Rabbis* (*Sifra l.c.*) the expression תפנו is to be understood in a wider sense. "Turn not", they say, "to worship them" (contrary to R. Judah, who holds that even turning the face towards idols—the mere looking at them—is forbidden). Cf supra p 142 and note 24.

Lev. 19, 14: "Thou shalt not curse the deaf, nor put a stumbling-block before the blind".

A. Clarke makes the following observation:—"The spirit and design of these two precepts are, that no man shall in any case take advantage of the ignorance, simplicity or inexperience of his neighbour". See also F. C. Cook and M. Mendelssohn l. c.

The Sadducees gave the verse a strict literal interpretation (cf. *Nid. 57a*), but the Rabbis understand the verse in a wider sense as referring also to typical figures of all misfortune, inexperience and moral weakness, (*Sanh. 66a; Sifra l.c.*) Cf. *Pes. 22b; Moed Ḳaṭan 5a, 17a; Ḳid. 32a; Ned. 62b; B. Meẓia 75b; Ḥul. 7b.* Cf. I. Abrahams, "Rabbinic Aids to Exegesis" (in Cambridge Biblical Essays 1909). Cf. supra p. 156 and note 18.

Num. 2, 20: "ועליו שבט מנשה"

In the Mishnah (*Men. 96a*) the Rabbis emphasise that על does not always mean "upon" but in some instances may also mean בסמוך (close to, by) for which they cite ועליו in above context. Cf. Gesenius K. §119cc. Similarly the word is rendered by the A. V. "And by him" and by the R. V. "And next unto him". The Rabbinic interpretation may also account for the rendering of Targum Onk., (followed by Rashi) "and those who were close to him"; cf. Pesh. which adds והחונים before ועליו and see G. B. Gray and Rashi ad loc. English translation ed. by A. M. Silbermann, note 1 Cf. supra p. 115 and note 86.

Num. 3, 10: "and the stranger that cometh nigh shall *be put to death*".

The word זר mentioned here and in many other places "does not mean a 'foreigner', but one who does not belong to the particular class mentioned in the context . . . Levites . . . the Priests", A. H. McNeile; see also G. B. Gray, ad loc. So too the *Rabbis in Shab. 31a* explain that the word זר in this text includes even David, the King of Israel, since, not being a descendant of Aaron, he was not of the priestly class. Cf. supra p. 142 and note 24.

Num. 3, 39: "twenty and two thousand".

Since this number of 22,000 Levites falls short by 300 of the total of the separate divisions mentioned in this chapter, some scholars read שלש for שש in v. 28 i.e., "three" hundred for "six" hundred; see A. H. McNeile and G. B. Gray. The Rabbis (*Bek. 5a*), followed by Rashi, Ibn Ezra, M. Mendelssohn, and some modern commentators (see C. J. Ellicott and F. C. Cook ad loc.) suggest that 300 of the Levites were firstborn and therefore not available for redeeming the firstborn of the other tribes, and accordingly their number is deducted from the total; see Num. 3, 45-46. Cf. supra p. 160 and note 51.

Num. 4, 3: "From thirty years old and upward . . .

Ancient and modern commentators draw attention to the discrepancy between this text and the later text (Num. 8, 24) where the minimum age prescribed for Levitical service is twenty five years (cf. Clarke, McNeile, Gray). This point is also dealt with by the Rabbis who explain thus: "From twenty five years on he (the Levite) comes to learn (i.e., the laws regulating the service) and at the age of thirty he may actually do the service", *Ḥul. 24a; Sifre ad loc.* Cf. Rashi, Ibn Ezra, RaMBaN, and M. Mendelssohn on Num. 8, 23. Cf. supra p. 160 and note 48.

Num. 4, 20: "ולא יבוא לראות כבלע את הקודש"

There is considerable diversity of opinion about the meaning of the expression כבלע. Targ. Onk., followed by Rashi, Ibn Ezra, Ḳimḥi, M. Mendelssohn, A. V. and A. Clarke, renders it in the sense of "Wrapping up" i.e., the

Kohathites are not to look at the Holy things while the latter are "wrapped up". Gesenius, however, (s.v. בלע) gives to this text a novel interpretation. He takes the word in its original sense ("to swallow") but as being used elliptically for the phrase ("swallow down spittle") with the same meaning as in Job 7, 19: "While I swallow down my spittle"—viz. a figurative expression for "the least moment of time". Accordingly, the meaning of the text is "neither shall they come in to see the Holy things (כבלע) even for a moment". The idea of this rendering of the text, given also in the R. V. and followed by F. C. Cook, has been anicipated by the Rabbis: "What, said R. Levi, is meant by כבלע? If they look upon the ark even for the twinkling of the eye" (*Num. R. 5, 9; Tanḥ. Vayak.* 7). Cf. supra p. 156 and note 18.

Num. 5, 15: "קרבנה . . . קמח שעורים"

The Rabbis (*Sifre ad loc.; cf. soṭa 15a*), contrasting the term קמח (coarse meal) used in this text, with סולת (fine meal) usually employed in connection with other meal offerings, make the following observation: "Because she (the suspected woman) committed a bestial act, therefore shall her offering consist of that which is food for beasts". While ingenious explanations are offered by some commentators to account for the nature of this offering which was of the cheapest and coarsest kind of meal (cf. A. H. McNeile and G. B. Gray ad loc.), the Rabbinic explanation is followed by Rashi, Ibn Ezra, and F. C. Cook who says: "The offering was to be of . . . barley representing the abased condition of the suspected woman". See J. H. Hertz ad loc. cf. supra p. 148 and note 13.

Num. 5, 17: מים קדשים "holy water".

This expression, regarded by some scholars as unique, has given rise to conjectural emendation as מים חיים, see A. H. McNeile and G. B. Gray. But the Rabbis (*Sifre ad loc.*) explain quite simply that "מים קדשים can only mean water that has become holy through being in the laver which stood near the Altar", thus מים קדשים denotes 'consecrated water', an explanation accepted by most of the modern commentators. Cf. supra p. 142 and note 24.

Num. 5, 18: "ופרע את ראש האשה"

There are two Rabbinic interpretations on the term פרע.

(1) "To let loose" (*Soṭa 8a*); so R.V.

(2) "To uncover" (*Sifre*). So A. V. Cf. Malbim, G. B. Gray and C. J. Ellicott ad loc. Cf. supra p. 98 and note 78.

Num. 5,18: "מי המרים"

The A. V. rendering "the bitter water", agrees with the interpretation in *Soṭa 20a;* cf. also *Sifre ad loc.* While the R. V. rendering "water of bitterness" would appear to be in accord with that in *Sifre ad loc.* where מי המרים is interpreted as a figure of speech i.e., water which produces woeful results, followed by Targ. Onk., Rashi and M. Mendelssohn. Cf. Ibn Ezra (who prefers the first interpretation), Malbim, A. H. McNeile, and G. B. Gray ad loc. Cf. supra p. 156 and note 18.

Num. 19, 2: "פרה אדמה תמימה"

According to Targ. Jon., followed by Ibn Ezra, the adjective תמימה "perfect" qualifies "heifer". Rashi, followed by M. Mendelssohn, takes the term as qualifying אדמה "red", i.e., wholly red; so, according to A. Clarke, the E. V. "without spot" which, he says, means "having no mixture of any other colour".

This agrees with the following Rabbinic reasoning: "Perfect in redness. It cannot imply blemish of the body, since the text expressly enjoins this in the following words", *Sifre l.c.* Cf. G. B. Gray and J. R. Dummelow. Cf. supra p. 98 note 78.

Num. 35, 33: "ולארץ לא יכפר"

According to the Rabbinic interpretation, the term לארץ implies "to the inhabitants of the land", cf. Sifre l.c., Keth. 37b; Soṭa 47b. See M. Mendelssohn ad loc. Cf. supra p. 162 and note 62.

Deut. 1, 17b: "לא תגורו מפני איש"

The meaning of תגורו according to the interpretation in *Sanh. 6b* is, "Ye shall not fear" with which Targ. Onk., E. V., and all modern commentators agree. According to another interpretation given by the Rabbis (ibid 7a) the word תגורו is to be explained on the analogy of אוגר ("gather in") in Prov. 10, 5, the meaning of the verse being: "Ye shall not hold back your words because of any man"—an interpretation preferred by M. Mendelssohn as being philologically inherent in the text. Cf. supra p. 134 and note 9.

Deut. 6, 4: "שמע ישראל ד' אלהינו ד' אחד"

Most commentators agree with the R. V. marg. that there are four possible translations of this text "The Lord our God the Lord One". The Rabbis, however, treating it as an ellipsis, render it: 'Hear, O Israel: the Lord is our God, the Lord is One', i.e., as J. H. Hertz remarks, "It sums up the teaching of the First and Second Commandments; the Lord is our God, and He is One". Cf. *Sifre ad loc.* Cf. supra p. 162 and note 62.

Deut. 6, 7a: ושננתם *"And thou shalt teach them diligently".*

ושננתם, "Lit. whet or sharpen . . . make incisive and impress them on thy children", G. A. Smith.

The rendering 'diligently' by the E. V., as explained above, agrees with the Rabbinic interpretationin *Ḳid. 30a,* "ושננתם that the words of the Torah shall be clear-cut (מחודדים) in your mouth, so that if anyone asks you something, you should not show doubt and then answer him, but (be able to) answer him immediately", deriving thus ושננתם from שנן, cf. Sifre ad loc., and also Ibn Ezra, RaSHBaM and M. Mendelssohn. See also A. Clarke who, however, explains "ושננתם" from שנן to repeat, iterate, or to do a thing again and again". Cf. supra p. 134 and note 9.

Deut. 18, 9: "Thou shalt not learn to do (לעשות) *after abominations of those nations".*

The Rabbis (*Ab. Zarah 43b; Sanh. 68b a.e.*), stressing the use here of the word לעשות "to do", observe "but thou mayest learn in order to understand and teach".[1]

1 That is to say, to understand their doings, how depraved they are, and thus to be able to teach thy children, 'do not so and so because these are the religious observances of the heathens', Rashi on Deut. 18, 9.

Deut. 21, 23: "כי קללת אלהים תלוי"

There is wide diversity of interpretation amongst commentators as to the meaning of this text (cf. F. C. Cook,

A. Clarke, and G. A. Smith). In the *Mishnah Sanh. 6, 6* we find three distinct interpretations. Perhaps the most interesting of all is the one given in the *Talmud* (*ibid 46b*). "To what is this matter comparable, R. Meir said, to two twin brothers (who lived) in one city; one was appointed King, and the other took to highway robbery. At the King's command they hanged him. But all who saw him exclaimed, 'The King is hanged!' whereupon the King issued a command and he was taken down". Accordingly deriving קללה from קל (cf. Rashi Deut. 21, 23) the meaning of the text is: "For he that is hanged is a קללת אלהים" i.e., a degradation of the Divine King, for man is made in His image; see M. Mendelssohn who adopts this interpretation as Peshaṭ. Cf. supra p. 134 and note 9.

Deut. 24, 7: "והתעמר בו"

והתעמר found only here and Deut. 21, 14. Targ. Onk., followed by RaSHBaM, renders it in the sense of 'trading'; similarly A. V. 'merchandise'. But according to the Rabbis, (*Sanh. 85b; Sifre l.c.*) followed by Rashi, the meaning of the word is "to employ as a slave"; similarly R. V. "deal with him as a slave". Similarly G. A. Smith on the use of the word in Deut. 21, 14, "The Hebrew verb seems only to mean to deal with her as her owner", and so S. R. Driver, "play the master over her", and cf. RaMBaN ad loc. Cf. supra p. 141 and note 3.

Deut. 25, 8: "Then the elders of his city shall call him, and speak unto him; ועמד ואמר".

The word ועמד is taken by the Targums, Sifre l.c. and by Rashi as the apodosis i.e., literally "and he shall stand". The E.V. and modern commentators take it figuratively, as the "continuation of the protasis of the 2nd sentence which starts in v. 7; the apodosis begins with v. 9", G. A. Smith. Thus the expression signifies 'and if he stands to it' and say . . . This agrees with the Rabbinic interpretation of the text in *Moed Ḳaṭan 21a* and *Yeb. 103a,* cf. M. Mendelssohn. Cf. supra p. 156 and note 18.

Deu.t 25, 19: "Thou shalt blot out the remembrance of Amalek".

For the full implication of the word זכר, Ibn Ezra, J. R. Dummelow l.c. refer to 1 Sam. 15, 3, where Samuel says to Saul: "Utterly destroy all that they have . . . slay . . . ox and sheep, camel and ass". See also Ḳimḥi on 1 Sam. 15, 3. The same interpretation and the same reference is given by the Rabbis in *Sifre* l.c. Cf. *B. Bathra 21b* referring to the correct vocalisation of this word, that it is זֵכֶר and not זָכָר. Cf. supra p. 110 and note 28; and pp. 159-160 and note 45.

Deut. 29, 8: "למען תשכילו"

The term תשכילו "deal wisely" (R.V. marg.), is rendered by the Rabbis (*Ab. Zarah 19b*) "to prosper". This is followed by the Targums, and Ibn Ezra and agrees with the E.V. So G. A. Smith and Ḳimḥi 1 Sam. 18, 14. Cf. supra p. 142 and note 24.

Jud. 2, 1:—"And an angel of the Lord came up from Gilgal".

The E.V. render the term מלאך in this text "angel". The Rabbis, however, on the analogy of Hag. 1, 13 ויאמר חגי המלאך במלאכות ד' "Then spoke Haggai, the Lord's messenger, in the Lord's message", render it 'prophet', (*Lev. R. 1, 1*). This is followed by A. Clarke ad loc. cf. supra pp. 159-160 and note 45.

1 Sam. 2, 24: "Nay my sons; for it is no good report that I hear מעבירים את עם ד'".

The margin in R.V., preferred by Kirkpatrick, renders the last clause "which I hear the Lord's people do spread abroad". This agrees with the Targums followed by Rashi. From the discussion in *Shab. 55b,* however, it appears that the Rabbis interpreted this text as follows: Ye make the Lord's people "transgress"—an interpretation followed by E. V. and by several commentators, and regarded by the Pulpit Commentary as "upon the whole, the best rendering". Cf. S. R. Driver, ad loc. Cf. supra p. 142 and note 24.

1 King. 11, 29: ". . . When Jeroboam went out of Jerusalem, that the prophet Ahijah the Shilonite found him in the way; and he (והוא) *had clad himself with a new garment".*

Commentators differ as to who is referred to by the pronoun הוא ('he') in this text. Ewald considers that it is Jeroboam and would see in the new garment his "splendid robe of office"; C. F. Burney takes the reference to be to Ahijah. (The Sept. and the Pesh. so R. V. read ואחיה instead of והוא). In *Ruth R. 7, 12* the Rabbis debate the question: "Whose garment was it?" Varying opinions are advanced by Rab, Levi and Samuel, the latter taking the reference to be to Ahijah. Cf. supra p. 98 note 78.

Is. 26, 19: "For thy dew is as the dew of herbs (אורות".

Ḳimḥi takes אורות in this text as having the same meaning as in 2 King. 4, 39 i.e., "herbs"; so E. V. The Rabbis in *Keth. 111b,* however, treating the expression טל אורות as a figure of speech, render it in its usual sense "lights" i.e., "for a dew of lights is thy dew". They are followed by Targ., Syr., Jerome, Rashi, Ibn Ezra (Friedlander's ed.), margin of R. V., Delitzsch and T. K. Cheyne. As J. Skinner remarks: "The word אורות means 'herbs' in 2 King. 4, 39, but the idea is too prosaic for this passage . . ." Cf. supra p. 156 and note 18.

Ps. 51, 19: "The sacrifices of God are a broken spirit (רוח נשברה)".

The style and idea expressed in this text are compared by critics with Is. 57, 15, and since the usual phrase is רוח שפלה it is suggested that originally our text was also שפלה instead נשברה as in Is. ibid; cf. F. Delitzsch and Z. P. Chajes (Heb. ed. by A. Kahana) ad loc. It is of interest to note that the *Rabbis* (*Sanh. 43b*) paraphrase this expression as meaning "humble in spirit". The rendering of the E. V. "broken spirit" is interpreted by A. F. Kirkpatrick, (in 'The Cambridge Bible for Schools & Colleges', Cambridge, 1901) ". . . the obstinacy of pride has been replaced by the humility of penitence". Cf. supra pp. 159-160 and note 45.

Ps. 139, 17: "How precious also are thy thoughts (רעיך) *unto me".*

Ḳimḥi, followed by the E. V., renders the word רעיך "thy thoughts". The Rabbis in *Lev. R. 2, 1,* however, take this word in its usual sense "thy friends" i.e., "how precious are thy friends unto me". This interpretation agrees with the rendering by the Sept. and, according to Z. P. Chajes, (Heb. ed. by A. Kahana), derives support from the contrasting context in v. 21, viz. "Do not I hate them O Lord, that hate Thee?" Cf. supra p. 159 and notes 40-2.

Job 21, 11: "They send forth their little ones (עויליהם) *like a flock . . ."*

The term עויליהם found only here and in Job 19, 18, is interpreted by some commentators as "their wicked little children", Lange; cf. also Pulpit Commentary on Job 19, 18 probably on the basis of Theod. and Vulg. which incorrectly have אוילים with an א; cf. Fuerst s.v. עויל. The E. V. and the majority of modern commentators give the same meaning as the Rabbis, who explain the word thus: "In Arabia they call a child Avila", *Gen. R. 36; Lev. R. 5, 1.* See International Critical Commentary, where this Rabbinic text is quoted by S. R. Driver and G. B. Gray. Cf. supra p. 136 and note 23.

Koh. 1, 14: ". . . all is vanity ורעות רוח"

This phrase רעות רוח, which occurs seven times in Koh., has been variously rendered by the Versions. The rendering by the A. V. "vexation of spirit", from רוע to break, is generally disapproved; see J. Lloyd, T. Taylor and C. H. H. Wright, whose rendering agrees with the Rabbinic interpretation of the word רעות as meaning "ambition", "striving", (cf. Gesenius Heb. and Chald. Lex. s.v.) i.e., "striving after wind", *Lev. R. 3, 1.* This is also followed by the R. V.; cf. supra p. 134 and note 9.

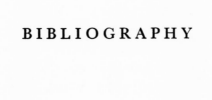

BIBLIOGRAPHY

RABBINIC SOURCES

Jerusalem Talmud (Piotrkow, 1899).

Babylonian Talmud (Wilna, 1887).

Mekilta (Vienna, 1870).

Sifra (Wilna, 1845).

Sifre (Vienna, 1864).

Midrash Rabbah (Wilna, 1884).

Yalkuṭ (Venice, 1566).

Tanḥuma (Buber's ed. Lemberg, 1885).

Talmudic references and quotations are to the Babylonian Talmud unless otherwise stated.

Translations of talmudic and midrashic sources are usually taken from the publications of the Soncino Press, though with some modifications, where required.

These publications are:

(1) Talmud Babli: The Soncino Press, London, 1935. (edited by I. Epstein).

(2) Midrash Rabbah: The Soncino Press, London, 1939. (edited by H. Freedman, and M. Simon).

LIST OF WORKS REFERRED TO:

(a) *Biblical Commentaries,* by the following:

Barnes, W. E.
Briggs, C. A.
Burney, C. F.
Chajes, Z. P.
Cheyne, T. K.
Clarke, A.
Cook, F. C.
Delitzsch, F.
Driver, S. R.
Dummelow, J. R.
Ellicott, C. J.
Ewald, G. H. A.
Gray, G. B.
Gordon, A. L.
Gordon, S. L.
Hertz, J. H.
Hitzig, F.
Ibn Ezra, A.
Jennings, A. C.
Kahana, A.
Keil, K. F.
Ḳimḥi, D.
Kirkpatrick, J. A. F.
Lloyd, J.
Malbim, M. L.
McNeile, A. H.
Mecklenburg, J. H.
Mendelssohn, M.
Naḥmanides, (RaMBaN).

Norzi, J. S. (Minḥath Shai).
RaLBaG, (commonly known as Gersonides).
RaSHBaM.
Rashi.
Ryle, H. E.
Skinner, J.
Smith, G. A.
Smith, R. P.
Spurrell, G. J.
Streane, A. W.
Tyler, T.
Wright, C. H. H.
Cambridge Bible for Schools and Colleges.
Pulpit Commentary.
The International Critical Commentary.
Westminster Commentaries.

(b) *Miscellaneous:*

Abrahams, I.: "Short History of Jewish Literature", London, 1906.

Abrahams, I.: "Rabbinic Aids to Exegesis", (Essay in Cambridge Biblical Essays, London, 1909).

Adret, Solomon b. Abraham, (RaSHBa); Novelae on the Talmud.

Albo, J.: "Iḳḳarim", Warsaw, 1877.

Baker, J.: "Work on D. Ḳimḥi", (unpublished).

Bamberger, S. B. (Heb. name I.D.): "Ḳore be-Emeth", Frankfurt a.M. 1871.

Ben-Ze'eb, J. L.: "Talmud Leshon Ibri", Wilna, 1879.

Box, G. H.: "Introduction" to Sifre on Numbers by P. P. Levertoff, London, 1926.

Chajes, Z. H.: "Introduction to the Talmud", Zolkiev, 1845.

Dei Rossi: "Meor Enayim", Vienna, 1829.

Deutsch, E.: "Literary Remains", London, 1874.

Enoch, Zundel b. Joseph: "Eẓ Joseph" (Commentary on the 'En Jacob', Wilna, ed.).

Epstein, B.: "Maḳḳor Baruk", Wilna, 1928.

Epstein, B.: "Torah T'mimah", Wilna, 1904.

Farrar, F. W.: "History of Interpretation", London, 1886.

Frankel, Z.: "Darke ha-Mishnah", Warsaw, 1923.

Friedlander, M.: "The Jewish Religion", London, 1937.

Friedlander, M.: "Essays on Ibn Ezra", London, 1877.

Gesenius: "Hebrew Grammar", (as ed. by Kautzsch, revised by A. E. Cowley), Oxford, 1910.

Graetz, H.: "History of the Jews", (Heb. ed. S. P. Rabinovitz), Warsaw, 1893.

Hagiz, M.: "Eleh ha-Mitzvoth", Wandsbeck, 1713.

Halevy, I.: "Doroth ha-Rishonim", Frankfurt a.M., 1918.

Hasting, J.: "The Greater Men and Women of the Bible", London, 1913.

Heidenheim, W.: "Habanath ha-Miḳrah", (Commentary on Rashi on the Pent.)

Heller, Yom-Ṭob Lipman: "Tosefoth Yom-Ṭob", (Commentary on the Mishnah).

Herford, R. T.: "Pharisees", London, 1924.

Herford, R. T.: "Talmud and Apocripha", London, 1933.

Horowitz, I.: "Shelah" (של"ה), Jozefov, 1878.

Hurwitz, P. E.: "Sefer ha-Berith", Warsaw, 1889.

Jolles, J.: "Melo Haroim", Halberstadt, 1859.

Judah ha-Levi: "Cuzari", Zamosc, 1796.

Krochmal, N.: "Moreh Nebuke ha-Zeman", Lemberg, 1863.

Landau, M.: "Pithron Hamiloth", Prague, 1827.

Levinsohn, I. B.: "Te'uddah Beyisroel", Warsaw, 1878.

Levinsohn, I. B.: "Beth Yehudah", Warsaw, 1878.

Lipschutz, I.: "Tifereth Yisrael", (Commentary on the Mishnah).

Maimonides, M.: "Introduction to the Mishnah".

Maimonides, M.: "Sefer Hamitzvoth".

Maimonides, M.: "Guide", (M. Friedlander's translation), 2nd ed., London, 1904.

Malbim, M. L.: "Commentaries on the Mek., Sifra, and Sifre".

Mielziner, M.: "Introduction to the Talmud", N.Y., 1925.

Nieto, D.: "Cuzari Ḥeleḳ Sheni", London, 1714.

Porter, J. S.: "Principles of Textual Criticism", London, 1848.

Rabinowitz, J.: "Mishnah Meg.", London, 1931.

Rosenblatt, S.: "Bible Interpretation in the Mishnah", Baltimore, 1935.

Rosenfield, S.: "Mishpaḥath Soferim", Wilna, 1883.

Ryle, H. E.: "The Canon of the Old Testament", London, 1904.

Schechter, S.: "Studies in Judaism", Philadelphia, 1945.

Schechter, S.: "Some Aspects of Rabbinic Theology", N.Y., 1909.

Schechter, S.: Documents of Jewish Sectaries", Cambridge, 1910.

Silbermann, A. M.: "Edited Rashi on the Pent. and translated into English", London, 1929.

Singer, S.: "The Authorised Daily Prayer Book", London.

Smith, W. R.: "Old Testament in the Jewish Church", London, 1895.

Stanley, A. P.: "History of the Jewish Church", London, 1890.

Strashun, S.: "Annotations on the Talmud".

Streane, A. W.: "Ḥagigah", (trans. into English), Cambridge, 1891.

Taylor, C.: "Sayings of the Jewish Fathers", Cambridge, 1877.

Weiss, I. H.: "Dor", Wilna, 1911.

Wright, D.: "The Talmud", London, 1932.

Wright, W.: "Comparative Grammar of Semitic Languages", Cambridge, 1890.

Zweifel, L.: "Sanegor", Warsaw, 1885.

In addition various articles in the following Encyclopedias and Reviews:

Jewish Encyclopedia.

Jewish Quarterly Review.

Journal of Theological Studies, London.

Hashiloaḥ, Cracow.

Ha-Oẓar, Hebrew and Chald. Dictionary, Warsaw, 1929, J. S. Fuenn.

Hebrew and Chald. Lexicon, London, 1846, Gesenius.

Heb. and Chald. Lexicon, London, 1871, J. Fuerst.

Dictionary of the Talmudic, Targ., and Midrashic Literature, London, 1926, M. Jastrow.

Kitto's Cyclopaedia of Biblical Literature.

Kokebe Yiẓḥaḳ, (Heb. Periodical ed. by M. Stern, Vienna).

Sefer Hamilim, Heb. Concordance, Wilna, 1908.

Oẓar Yisroel, Hebrew Encyclopedia.

The Expositor, London.